# A Life For Lucy

**A Life For Lucy**
**The touching true story of a wild dog's journey to happiness.**

iUniverse books may be ordered through booksellers or by contacting:

iUniverse
1663 Liberty Drive
Bloomington, IN 47403
www.iuniverse.com
1-800-Authors (1-800-288-4677)

The views expressed in this work are solely those of the author and do not necessarily reflect
the views of the publisher, and the publisher hereby disclaims any responsibility for them.

ISBN: 978-1-4401-1606-3 (pbk)
ISBN: 978-1-4401-1615-5 (ebk)

Printed in the United States of America

Edited by Derek Bowyer.
Design and Artwork by Jennifer Quinn.
Photography by Derek Bowyer Jnr. and Suzie Brown

iUniverse rev. date: 12/17/2008

To my husband.
I am. You are. It is.

# The Author

I was born in England and moved to Banada in County Sligo, Ireland in 1998 with my husband Derek, and our two children, Derek Junior and Suzanne. We purchased an old secluded cottage together with six acres of land.

My passion for dogs began when I was three years old and living with an aunt and uncle, who bred and showed Bedlington Terriers and Fox Terriors.

Throughout my life I have always been involved with dogs, whilst at the same time pursuing, up to my early twenties, a career in nursing, both general and psychiatric. I then changed direction entirely to become a qualified driving instructor, running my own business for three years from the service station that Derek and I had in the UK.

My careers have run alongside and complemented my present work, because each has enabled me to draw from experiences with so may different people and their individual needs, strengths and weaknesses.

Now approaching my sixties, I am lucky enough to be able to work with people and their dogs on an individual basis, in the beauty of my home surroundings.

I am a canine psychologist and dog trainer and have studied with the Canine behaviour Centre (UK), the Animal Care College (UK) and am a professional member of the Institute of Animal Care Professionals (USA).

My hobbies are training and working with dogs, walking and writing.

www.one2onedogs.com

# 1

The date – Wednesday 22nd March 2006. As I woke up to the annoying sound of the alarm, advising me that it was 6.30am and time to rise, I really had no idea as to what the day had in store for me, or how it would affect me, in both my knowledge of and my relationship with dogs. Little did I realise that I was about to embark on a journey that would take me to emotional highs and lows, test my patience to the very limit, and make me realise how much more there still was to learn about man's best friend – the dog.

The day, as usual, had started with the mandatory morning cup of tea and a quick look at the TV news to check the weather forecast for the day. Meanwhile I was being watched most closely by two pair of eager eyes belonging to my two Border Collies, Sunny, who is six and Jimmy, who is three. The reason for the close and unblinking scrutiny was that I was being told it was time for the morning run across the bog lands and through the forestry.

On these walks the only sounds that could be heard were those of the hundreds of birds that shared the idyll with us, and as it was nearing April, the repetitive call of the cuckoo could be heard close by, announcing his presence and making us aware that spring had arrived at last.

I very often stood for a while during the morning walk and took time out just to listen. I could identify different bird calls; listen to a donkey braying in the distance, the sound of cows on a farm, across the bog land, calling to the farmer for their early morning feed. I knew that kinder weather was on its way, when I was accompanied on part of my journey by the endless croaking of the frogs. I came across massive pools of frogspawn. There must be literally thousands in the area, and we often got them coming onto our outside patio, right up to the back door. That could prove to be very amusing, as Sunny was scared of them. He would investigate one, but if it should jump whilst he was doing that, I guarantee that Sunny would definitely leap a lot higher.

I never took for granted the natural beauty of all the things that surrounded me; I followed the dogs' example. They would stop and sniff, or perhaps just stare out across the heather, so I would stop too and was always amazed at the variety of sights and sounds that could be seen and heard. There was the aroma of coconut when the gorse began to bloom and the earthy smell of the scuffed up peat and moss. I would have missed all that if I hadn't joined the dogs in their quiet moments and taken the time just to reflect. It was the highlight of the dogs' day, running free, no restrictions, new scents to follow and sometimes the added bonus of a hare or fox to chase after. Now whilst Sunny was always happy to take an active part in the chase, Jimmy would supervise from the sidelines. Not the most energetic of dogs, he had learnt that the best way to start his day was by sauntering along at my side, occasionally drifting off to examine something in the undergrowth, but not going for too long. I loved the morning walk, which I do every day of the year, as it afforded me the time to gather my thoughts together.

Every day is a busy day, so I have to plan the time carefully, to allow for training sessions that have been booked, household tasks and the inevitable shopping. The morning walk occupied the first hour and a half of the day, and I arrived back at the cottage by half past eight, where my husband Derek had got things organised ready for breakfast. I then had time to set about feeding the goats, sheep, hens and ducks and quickly muck out the sheds that needed it. Then, it was back indoors, upstairs for a shower and down again for breakfast, which had been prepared by him who was to be obeyed in the kitchen. The kitchen was Derek's territory, for which I was extremely grateful, as cooking was never one of my favourite pastimes.

My first lesson of the day was due to start at ten thirty, with another following an hour later. With luck I would be finished before 1 o'clock.

I had just come to the end of my second session when my mobile phone rang. It was a call from a local rescue centre asking me if I could possibly go over to them and assess two dogs, that had been part of a pack of some thirteen dogs, all totally feral, kept in thoroughly appalling conditions, without any form of human contact. I did not actually witness the horror of their situation when they were first discovered, but I was given to understand that food was just tossed in to them, and they were left to fend for themselves. In essence, they were a pack of wild dogs.

It sounded like a challenge, as eleven of the pack had already been euthanized by the attending veterinary surgeon, Darren Carr. They had been able to capture the two remaining smaller dogs. It transpired that they had been sent on to another larger rescue centre for a month, but no one there had been able to do anything with them. They remained as feral as the day they were found and so they had been sent back to the original rescue centre to be put to sleep.

When I arrived at the shelter I was taken to their pen. I saw immediately that the two dogs were petrified and looked totally lost in these unfamiliar surroundings. One of the dogs was a medium size black and white Collie/cross, and the other was a smaller white and tan Collie/cross. I set about assessing the two dogs but realised, after an hour, that there would never be any possibility of them being re-homed in the usual manner. I would never be able to explain why, even if my life depended on it, why something about them touched me deeply at that moment in time, so much so that I asked the people at the shelter if they would delay any final decision until the following day.

I realised that I already knew what I wanted to do, but the question that needed an answer was how and where?

The journey home was about twenty miles which gave me time to think out the various options. When I got back to the cottage, Derek asked me how the assessment went, so I told him that I didn't think that there was anything that could be done for them and for that moment left it there. I did have many thoughts that I wanted to share with him about the situation, but that would be better addressed in the evening when we were settled in the lounge. So later on, I tentatively voiced my thoughts to him, keeping everything possible crossed in the hope that he would support my decision to bring the two girls back to our home. It was at that point, speaking my thoughts out loud to him, that I began to question my sanity. Derek, true to form, said that he would do all he could to help, but it would be up to me to deal with the day to day situation in the best way that I could. Up to that point I had been involved with dogs for over twenty eight years, but had never been faced with a challenge like that before.

Sleep did not come easily that night, as my thoughts were a complete jumble and a thousand and one questions kept flashing through my mind, so many questions and so few answers at that stage. I was relieved when morning finally dawned and I could put the night behind me.

The very first thing that I had to do on the Thursday morning was to telephone the shelter and tell them of my decision. They said that they were delighted that something could be done, but I wondered whether they secretly thought to themselves that here was yet another example of the mad English and their attitude to dogs. Derek and I then discussed the various arrangements that would need to be made to accommodate the two girls. We were really left with no other choice than to try to do something with the smaller of our two mobile homes, which hitherto had only ever been used as a standby for the occasional visitor. It was fully equipped, together with electricity, water, etc. and with a few alterations regarding security, could be made into a suitable holding area for the time being, whilst the dogs were getting settled and becoming used to the presence of human company. It had to be borne in mind that the dogs had not received any human contact whatsoever and any food given to them had been thrown over a wall into filthy disused sheds.

As the mobile home was carpeted, it would require some sort of protection, so Derek made a phone call to Roemer Furnishings in Sligo and spoke to Paul. He explained the situation about the rescue dogs and was told that we would be more than welcome to a good sized piece of vinyl that would cover the entire carpeted area. Paul said that there would be no charge, as it was for a good cause.

We made a quick trip to Sligo to collect it, as time was not really on our side. There was still much to do and not a lot of time to do it in, as the dogs were due to be brought down to us from the shelter the next day, which was the Friday afternoon.

On our return, we laid the floor covering down, cut it to a reasonable size to cover the carpet and a few inches up the walls. We removed all the soft furnishings that we could and put everything out of reach that might cause the dogs a problem. We constructed a gate across the entrance from the kitchen to the lounge. I put down a good supply of blankets for bedding, a suitable water dish and looking at the finished alterations, decided that I was then fully prepared. Just how wrong I was will be revealed as time goes on.

Added to that I then realised I was faced with yet another unforeseen problem that I could have done without. A few days earlier Sunny had been with me in the garden. There was nothing that he liked better than to chase a tennis ball and bring it back for a repeat throw. The game could last all day, if necessary, up until the time my energy ran out, which usually happened long before his ever did.

Anyway, in between my weeding I was throwing the ball over my shoulder, without any general sense of direction, and Sunny kept bringing it back. I love all my dogs dearly, but Sunny did have the annoying habit of carefully dropping the ball into any hole I had prepared for plants, which meant my gardening attempts seemed to go one step forward and two steps back. One more throw I thought and then it would be time to take the ball away, send him off indoors to Derek, then grab a few minutes of uninterrupted gardening. Just as I was thinking that, I threw the ball and a few seconds later heard the most piercing scream. I knew something was terribly wrong. I leapt to my feet, turned around and immediately saw that Sunny was drooling and pawing frantically at his mouth.

I could not for the life of me grasp what might have happened, until I realised that he was right next to a large rose bush. The ball had apparently landed in the centre of the bush, and Sunny had gone full pelt into the bush to grab the ball, missed it, but in the process had driven a large piece of the rose stem into the back of his mouth. The poor fellow was in so much pain, that I had to put a temporary muzzle on him, then rush to the nearest vet's surgery for some urgent attention. On arrival they ushered him straight in and said that they would have to anaesthetise him and that they would call me in the afternoon, once they had a chance to examine him more thoroughly. They did call later and said that I could rest assured that it was not too deep a puncture, that everything had been flushed out of the wound and that apart from having a sore mouth for a couple of days, he should be fine.

Unfortunately after three days he was still not his usual old self. He was not interested in running around and was having difficulty eating his food, unless it was softened first. So, there I was with two rescue dogs about to be unloaded on me and one of my old friends looking very sorry for himself. I knew that all was not as it should be, so it was then time to call on my own veterinary surgeon and good friend, Suzie Brown, from the Green Veterinary Clinic in Boyle, Co. Roscommon. The surgery was probably about 25 miles away, but we were talking about a journey along mainly quiet, but in places, very bumpy country roads.

During the journey Sunny continued to deteriorate, and as soon as Suzie saw him, she immediately recognised that he had tetanus. She sedated him, so that she could examine his mouth more thoroughly, and the examination revealed that the puncture wound was in fact quite deep. The wound was flushed out thoroughly and pieces of rose stem came out. At that stage

Sunny was having muscle spasms. Suzie gave him the tetanus antidote. She did explain to me that she could not be sure if the problem had been caught in time, but the best that could have been done, had been done. It was a worrying journey home because Sunny kept having spasms. The third eyelids were pronounced in his eyes and he really did look so miserable. Apart from feeling very upset at seeing him like that, I also felt guilty about having thrown the ball in the first place in such a random fashion, without looking to see where it was going to land. They say you are never too old to learn yet another lesson, but at what cost I wondered?

By the time we arrived back at the cottage with Sunny, it was past noon, so we left him in a darkened room on his own, as at first, he did not tolerate any movement near him, nor did he like the light, preferring the darkness and quiet. During the next few days his condition slowly improved. It was all of four weeks after that before he showed signs of anything like a full recovery and a return to his old self, then several more weeks before it could be said that he had finally made a full recovery.

To this day he will not let anyone touch his mouth, and he still does not like lights if they are bright. He also gets very irritable if he is out in the bright sunshine, and the third eyelids become evident in his eyes. It has to be said that without Suzie's quick assessment and treatment, I am sure that Sunny would not be with us today. A stressful start to the Friday then, the day of all days that things should have gone without a hitch. Our new arrivals were due inside of two hours and there was still such a lot of preparation to be done.

So off we went, armed with an assortment of food and water bowls, cleaning materials, towels, rubbish bags, kitchen rolls, rubber gloves, and a plentiful supply of coffee, tea and milk. I remember thinking at the time that I was so glad that we had kept the mobile home up together, although we never expected that it would be put to use in this manner.

Just after three o'clock the van from the shelter arrived, bringing the latest additions to the Bowyer clan.

Both dogs defecated and urinated as they were being carried on the way from the van to their new home. Not the best of starts.

We eventually got them into the safe area of the mobile home lounge and decided that it would then be best to leave them to their own devices, to give them a chance to settle into their new and unfamiliar surroundings. The folks from the shelter took their leave, when it then finally dawned on me that I was on my own, approaching what you might call unexplored territory. So, back at the cottage, where I sat for a few minutes with a hot drink, not really having any idea what might come next.

I returned to the mobile home at about five o'clock, and as I opened the door the first thing that greeted me was the terrible smell. A mixture of diarrhoea and very strong urine, mixed with the odour from their coats, assailed my nostrils. I stepped back outside and took a couple of deep breaths of fresh air, before entering again for a closer look. The floor was awash with urine and faeces, not only the floor, but up the walls and over the bedding that I had left. I stood for a moment, whilst the reality of what I had undertaken dawned on me. It was then time to go outside for more fresh air and a trip back to the cottage to put on my wellies and an old waterproof coat to protect my clothes.

Up until then I had been very careful not to make eye to eye contact, and I made sure that my body language, at all times, was non-threatening.

When I re-entered they were pacing frantically round and round. That made cleaning up extremely difficult as they were also spreading the mess everywhere, and everything I did had to be in slow motion. The tan and white dog, who we had decided to call Lucy, growled continuously and the black and white dog, now named Molly, was silent, which worried me more. I had no idea whether they might attack me in a confined space. I just hoped that my body language would continue to indicate that I meant no harm to them. As they were circling me I made sure that I was always facing them.

It took me over an hour to clear up the worst of the mess, so I then decided to leave them for a few minutes on their own, giving them a chance to calm down. Also another opportunity for me to take in some fresh air. I wen back to the cottage, checked on Sunny, fed Jimmy and my five elderly miniature Dachshunds, Solo, Archie, Jack, Billie and Carrie. Derek and I then had our evening meal. By the time that was finished and we had cleared up, it was time to go back to the mobile home and attend to the feeding of the new additions.

I prepared their food in the kitchen area, and I could see that what I was doing had evoked some interest. I put down two separate bowls of food and refilled the large water bowl, most of its previous contents having been spilt all over the floor.

I then stood back to observe what would happen. What a surprise... nothing. They just kept staring at me, so I went back to the door, turned to one side, and after a little while Lucy tentatively edged towards the food dish, with both her and Molly still fixing me with a stare. I felt that I would achieve nothing by continuing to stay in their presence, so I decided to leave them to it and come back again in an hour, when hopefully the food would be gone.

Just as I expected, when I returned later, the food was all gone, but the floor was awash again. I noticed then that the urine was blood stained and the smell was terrible. Something else I then noticed, that I had not seen before, was quite a large growth on one of Molly' back legs. That was something that would need attention before too long. They were both still extremely agitated and pacing about continuously. Whilst I was clearing up the mess, from the floor they both circled me, never taking their eyes off of me for one second. I had to make sure I did not let them come up to me from behind my back, so I had to continuously turn as they were circling me. This made my task of cleaning up very difficult and time consuming.

They kept urine marking, both of them cocking their legs like male dogs. Thank heavens for the vinyl. They marked everything that they could, food bowls, water bowl, even if I dropped a cloth or moved away from the bucket, they would mark that. Molly, the black and white did it all the time. I was using a few newspapers to try and avoid a paddling pool every time I went in, but I had to be very careful to keep the black bin liners out of their reach, when I was depositing dirty paper because Molly, given the chance, would urinate on them as well. There was a fixed seating unit halfway around the lounge. I had removed the cushions from it and just laid some blankets on the base. Molly marked this as well, although by the third day she ceased doing so. Up until then my washing machine had been working nonstop.

I made another visit late in the evening, just before ten o'clock, put fresh water down, turned off all the lights and went back to the cottage. It was a fine clear night, quiet under a starlit sky, and I reflected just for a moment on my first day. It somehow still did not seem to be real. Should I have taken more time, but no, that could not have been done, time was not an option, their lives had been in the balance.

Once back indoors I collapsed into the welcoming comfort of my chair by the fire and did a little more reflecting. They had only been with us for a matter of a few hours and already I was tired and worried. I realised that although there was only one choice that could have been made to try to guarantee the girls survival, who was I to say that the decision that I had made was necessarily the right one for them. Having now seen them close at hand and having spent several hours in their company it was obvious that they were truly feral dogs. For them to lead a normal relaxed life they would need to be rehabilitated. I knew that it was going to take months of hard work, commitment, seeking new methods of approaching the dogs and addressing their many problems.

I had to ask myself was Sunny going to be OK with them? Would the other dogs accept Molly and Lucy into their little household pack? Here we go again, more questions and another sleep disturbed night.

Fortunately our bedroom is equipped with tea making facilities, and that was something that we were both glad to take advantage of at about 3am, when sleep was still evading me. Derek didn't mind being woken up, seeing that I was in charge of making the tea. It made a welcome break for me to be able to talk with him and speak about my hidden fears. A troubled shared is a troubled halved, so I have been told, and I did feel that in this case the saying was very true.

# 2

---

I had already decided to get up an hour earlier each day, until I had established some sort of permanent routine, as I still had my own dogs to care for and a busy schedule of training sessions to fit in each day. The extra hour should then give me enough time to clear up the mobile home and spend a little while with the two new additions, hoping that they might begin to associate my presence with something pleasurable. I decided that it might be better to feed them two small meals a day, and I arranged for Suzie to send me over some antibiotics to help clear up the diarrhoea and urinary infections. Fortunately, they had been given their vaccinations previously at the animal shelter.

The next morning, as I approached the mobile home, they heard my footsteps on the gravel and started to bark and growl.

I felt that they were best ignored, so I entered, taking care not to make any eye contact and again made my moves very slow and deliberate. I was greeted by the now too familiar smell and mess, which was still terrible. It took a long time to clear up again. Whilst I was doing that they kept circling me, and unless my movements remained very slow, they soon became extremely agitated. Lucy growled and told me in no uncertain terms to back off. I put the food bowls and clean water down and was then able to retire to the kitchen area, behind the gate. I watched as Molly started to eat, but Lucy was snatching bits of food from the same bowl. Then Molly started on the other bowl and Lucy did the same thing again. Once the food had gone, Molly urinated in both bowls. I returned to the lounge and removed the bowls and that time they didn't circle me, but instead jumped up on to the area that they were using as their bed, half sitting on one another, never taking their eyes off of me for one moment.

That little session had taken an hour, so I left them to themselves and went back to the cottage for a cup of tea, before taking Jimmy on his morning walk. Sunny was still the same, seeking quiet and hiding away. Jimmy of course was completely oblivious to the entire goings on and the turmoil in my mind, as he found his favourite piece of turf and raced around flinging it into the air with not a care in the world! Dear Jimmy, such a clown, he could always be relied upon to lift my spirits, however low they might have been.

To put a time scale to events, it was then Sunday morning. I had been awake since about 4am planning my day, making a mental list of tasks to complete. I had already decided to have my first cup of tea each day in the mobile home with Molly and Lucy. I had left a comfortable armchair in the lounge area, suitably covered for protection. The plan was to take my cup of tea, sit down quietly and see what happened. I did notice, on entering, that the smell was not quite as strong, or perhaps I was just becoming used to it? No…there was less diarrhoea, but the floor was still very wet with urine.

Neither of them barked when I approached, but Lucy growled at anything other than very slow movement. I switched the kettle on, and as the water started to boil, I could see that they were becoming very agitated by the new sound. They started to pace back and forth continuously, so I made my tea, only filling the mug half way, in case they did anything, as I approached my chair, that might make me jump.

I had placed the chair more or less in the centre of the lounge so that they could go all the way around me, if they wanted to, but they took up their usual places on their bed area, sat and stared. As I slowly raised my cup to drink, Lucy started to growl in quite a threatening way, Molly meanwhile just stared. I took my time and sat quietly, slowly moving the cup and continued to observe them out of the corner of my eye. I had, until then, avoided any direct eye contact with either of them. I continued to remain motionless, apart from moving the cup to drink and kept that up for about 20 minutes. Lucy continued to growl, and I wondered how they would react when I finally got up from the chair. That question was soon answered. They reacted by jumping down from their rest area and started to circle me. Lucy then stopped growling, but neither of them took their eyes off of me.

I stood sideways by the barrier gate, and Lucy started to growl again. I did not move. After a few minutes she stopped growling, so I took the opportunity to leave them on their own for a while. As I passed by the lounge windows they both had their noses pressed against the glass, still obviously watching my every move.

Back at the cottage I made my way upstairs, where one of our windows overlooked the small mobile home, I saw immediately that they had settled down quietly, once left alone. Throughout the remainder of the day I spent short periods of time with them, most of which was taken up with cleaning. Molly was still cocking her leg and marking everything. Lucy was doing the same, but not quite as frequently. Whilst cleaning up I did notice that their behaviour had changed slightly. Lucy would pace up and down, whilst Molly would sit on the side and just stare. That she did without moving a single muscle, not a twitch, and I must admit that I found it more unnerving than Lucy's pacing.

I felt that it was time to try to encourage them into the training field, which was only a few feet away from the mobile home. I constructed a makeshift barrier from the mobile home door to the field gate, thus giving them the option of either going into the field, or back into the mobile home, the choice was theirs. I did not feel too confident at that stage because I could not approach them and had really no idea as to how agile they might prove to be. To put that into perspective, the chain link fencing around the training field was 4 feet high and Sunny could clear it with ease. In Jimmy's case that had never been a problem I had to contend with, as his idea of a jump was preferably not to. I opened the mobile home door and had the gate to the field already open, removed the barrier gate, then went back outside and waited. After a short while they ventured forth, both slunk down and were obviously very frightened at being outside.

I almost forgot to breathe as I watched every move. They immediately began scent marking, then after a few minutes Molly took off at the rate of knots around the field. She seemed delighted with her new found freedom. However, that was short lived, as after only a few moments of strenuous exercise, she collapsed on to the ground and appeared to be totally exhausted. I watched, waited and wondered how she was going to react should it be necessary for me to pick her up. That might present a problem. After what seemed like an eternity, but can only have been a few minutes, she recovered her composure and slowly got to her feet. They then both made their way back inside, to what was already becoming their safe haven.

Later that Sunday evening, after paying my last visit to them of the day, I returned to the cottage and felt totally tired and drained. They had been with us for only three days, so why did it feel like a month? I was also faced with the additional worry of people coming for lessons during the next week. I wondered how Molly and Lucy would react to people and their dogs passing by the mobile home, not something they would have experienced before. Would this unsettle them even more, would they be noisy? What if...what if... still too many questions and few answers. I just knew that there was another sleepless night ahead, but having said that, I could hardly remember having got into bed. I was absolutely exhausted. No cup of tea during the early hours, as I did not wake up until 5.30 am, when the alarm sounded.

Monday morning looked like it was going to be another fine day, as even that early, one could see a clear sky. So, after doing the usual early morning bits and pieces, I went over to the mobile home. I made sure that my barriers were still intact and then left the door open for them to go into the training field. They went without hesitation, and I was then able to clear up the lounge thoroughly, whilst they were outside enjoying the fresh scents of the day. It was much easier and far quicker clearing up without them being present, and it enabled me to spend over half an hour enjoying a hot drink in their company. I still could not relax totally at that stage because I found that even when sitting in my chair, the slightest movement of my foot would provoke a response from Lucy, who would immediately start to growl. Should I cough or sneeze both of them reacted, either by growling or pacing around me. By now I was perfecting the art of doing just about everything in slow motion.

Derek came over with me after lunch and went inside for the first time. The girls had not seen him before, and they remained silent and huddled together the whole time that he was there. At that stage I had not attempted to stroke either of them, so over the course of the next few days I spent time trying to encourage them to take a tasty titbit from my hand. I held the treat in my hand and sat and waited. I kept that up for a couple of days and, eventually, Lucy stretched out her neck like a giraffe and took the treat. That was as close as she came on that occasion, but I could tell that she was gentle. It took Molly considerably longer, but she eventually succumbed and took a treat, she too was very gentle.

The following day I wormed them both, as they still had bouts of diarrhoea and a presence of worms. I also started them on a course of antibiotics for the urinary infections and colitis. Later that day Derek spent an hour with them in the lounge just sitting quietly, and eventually they both took treats from his outstretched hand, which we counted as a huge step forward. In the evening Lucy let me stroke behind her ear and on her chest, but only for a few brief moments, and she then retired to her bed area. They still seemed to be settled, which was very encouraging.

Then it was time for the next step. I thought that I would try the vacuum cleaner. As soon as I switched it on the sudden noise obviously frightened them, but they were not out of control and soon settled again once the cleaner was switched off. I continued to stroke Lucy from time to time and she seemed to like that, but on her terms. Just a few seconds at a time, as if to say 'do not try and get too familiar'.

I did ask one of the ladies that I knew quite well to sit with them after her lesson, but they were extremely wary and reacted to every movement that she made, however slight. Tuesday and Wednesday followed more or less the same pattern as usual, but on the Thursday morning there was no clearing up to do first thing. That made the start to the day so much easier. They seemed to be agitated and uneasy when I left them, but when

I was out of sight they soon settled down again. They did bark and lunge at the lounge windows when people walked by with their dogs, which made me rather tense, as the big picture window in the lounge was only single glazed, in an aluminium frame. I had visions of them coming through and appearing outside.

I think that others might have had the same picture as they passed by, as I noticed their pace visibly quickened as they rounded the corner to the training shed, with their dog strung out at the end of the lead!

I carried on with their usual routine, once the last training sessions were over, and the days went smoothly enough.

On the Friday there was no mess again, so it would appear that we had moved on a step. The fact that clearing up now seemed to be in the past was a great improvement and allowed me to spend more quality time with them both of them. Apart from their individual distinctive smell, the air was definitely sweeter. So, to sum up…after a very hectic and uncertain start, they had settled in quite well in their first week.

It was now the last day of March and the beginning of a new week. Lucy liked to spend more time being stroked. Well, let us say that she tolerated it for about two minutes. Molly however still refused to be touched. I thought that I would try them with knuckle bones and immediately discovered that Molly had a more assertive personality.

I had to remove the bones on the afternoon visit, for fear that she might attack Lucy. The next morning I was very conscious that it was April 1st and being April Fool's day, felt perhaps the keyword for the day should be caution. However, both of the dogs seemed to be much more settled. Lucy actually seemed to really enjoy being stroked, and I was able to run my hand over her back and down her legs. I could see that Molly was also considering allowing me to stroke her, but was still reticent. I did tentatively and very briefly, manage to stroke her chest once, but that one stroke was all she permitted.

Each day now had developed into a more organised routine. They were both toilet trained by that time, but I had noticed that they both still scent marked continuously when they were outside. I also had to be careful that I did not leave anything different on the floor, as they would both mark it immediately. I discovered that Molly liked a rolled up sock to play with. When I first showed it to her she pawed at it, so I threw it on the floor, and she picked it up and took it away to her bed, but she then soon lost interest in it. Neither of them had ever had the advantage of learning puppy games and skills from people when they were young, so playing was not something that either of them would have experienced when growing up.

At the weekend I was able to spend more time with them, without neglecting Sunny and Jimmy and my oldies. The two girls were now feeding from separate bowls for the first time. I had to distract Lucy when she had finished her meal, otherwise she would home in on Molly's food, as Molly ate very slowly. No incidents for the remainder of that day which took me through to ...

Monday 3rd April.

I had a lovely greeting first thing that morning. The two girls seemed to be really excited to see me, and Molly even allowed me to stroke her, once I had sat down. She was also running after the sock three or four times before losing interest. I was amazed because she rolled over on her back to be tickled. Lucy remained aloof and would not permit such excesses at that time.

Each morning they seemed to be more and more excited to see me. I had been leaving a collar around for them to get used to, but unfortunately even the sight of it made them very agitated. I did take the opportunity of asking a couple of people that they didn't know, to sit in with them, but they became very tense and the slightest movement would provoke a reaction. If anyone came towards me they would both bark and growl in a very aggressive manner. They responded in the same way to a sneeze or cough, or if anyone spoke. I knew then that it was about time to try to remove them from their present environment, before they made it their domain. Up until then their world had been so very small.

Nothing much untoward happened over the course of the next few days, life for us went on more or less as normal. My lessons, a bit of local shopping and a few hours in Sligo town to allow me some time for a little retail therapy. Derek liked to have his morning tea and read his paper in the Southern Hotel, where we have always been made very welcome. Derek does not do shopping, for which I am eternally grateful, as I much prefer to take my time and enjoy the couple of hours break.

It was on the 14th of April, which was Good Friday, that a big step forward was taken. I introduced Lucy and Molly to Sunny and Jimmy. I let Sunny out first into our car parking area, as that was a more neutral area. Sunny approached both of the girls at great speed, but after much sniffing, seemed to be OK with them. Lucy looked very nervous and was giving all the body signals to advise any and all that she did not want any trouble. Molly just bristled, but didn't take it any further. I observed them for a few minutes, and then it was time to let Jimmy out. Once outside he appeared to be a little unsure. Jimmy had never possessed any social skills, and his reaction to other dogs was always very varied. However, he too did a lot of sniffing. Both Molly and Lucy reacted in the same way as they had done with Sunny, but all in all there were no problems in the thirty minutes or so that they were all together. I noticed that Molly had started to moult, I also noticed for the first time, that the front teeth on both of the girls had been worn completely away to gum level. I wondered if that had been caused by them gnawing away at the metal frame of the shed that they were found in originally. I felt that it was quite likely, as I could think of no other reason for the condition.

The following day I had both of the girls in the front garden with Sunny and Jimmy, whilst I caught up with some gardening. There was such a lot to do and unfortunately Derek was not able to do that type of work any more, due to his arthritis. He could however be persuaded to make the afternoon tea and bring that and the cakes into the garden. We had a quiet seat that was situated in the shade under two well established hawthorn trees, that was a quiet haven for us to enjoy together, with the dogs rallying around just in case there was a dropped crumb or two to be had.

I did however keep a watchful eye on the dogs' reactions to one another. I noticed that when Jimmy barked, which he did at almost any unusual sound, Molly reacted by squaring up and rushing towards him. Surprisingly, that brought no reaction whatever from Jimmy. To sum up then a very pleasant afternoon, without incident.

I was still being very cautious with my five elderly miniature long haired Dachshunds and had made no attempt to introduce them to Lucy and Molly. I had been made aware that there were dead animals in their previous habitat, and I had no doubts that the pack of feral dogs had been responsible. There would no doubt be a right time to make the introductions, but that was not a matter of urgency. Lucy seemed more relaxed with me now and she really liked to have her tummy rubbed. Occasionally she would paw the ground to indicate that she would like more of the same. She was still not letting anyone else near her. She appeared to be taking an interest in her surroundings and did not shut down so often. Molly was also sitting on command, so I asked them both to do that before I allowed them their food. I would gradually ask them for that behaviour before they got other pleasures.

The following day was a Sunday and providing the weather was favourable, that was the day that I liked to catch up on the many outside tasks that need to be done. One of the important issues was that of mowing the training field, as the grass had to be kept short. It was a fine warm day, so I decided to let the girls out, with Sunny and Jimmy. This time Molly kept challenging Sunny. Sunny told her off, and Jimmy of course had to join in by barking at her. She backed off when that happened, and all was fine between them for the rest of the day. The incident did leave me with an uneasy feeling, as I had never known any other dog challenge Sunny. So, the next day I repeated the move, but Molly made no attempt to challenge either Sunny or Jimmy again.

Over the course of the next couple of days the dogs appeared to be mixing well but I had noticed that Molly and Lucy growled and paced around in the mobile home, if there was anyone else in there with me.

# 3

---

Some friends of ours paid us a visit on the Wednesday afternoon, and I kept the girls outside so that they could keep their distance if they so wished. They were both very curious and did keep distance between them and the guests, but neither of them growled or barked. After a few minutes we all went into the mobile home, and I made coffee for everyone. At that stage Molly and Lucy shot past us and sat close together, in their usual place and did not take their eyes off of us. They were very quiet to start with, but if anyone moved, even slightly, Lucy started to growl. I did not want to put anyone at risk so I escorted our friends, one by one, very slowly out of the mobile home. I had noticed that the girls seemed more at ease, when others were present, providing I moved with them, but they had both started to exhibit threatening behaviour if someone approached me. With a view to further settling them down, I gave them each a large Kong filled with treats. That brought keen attention as there was the prospect of food to be found inside.

I left them totally engrossed with the new toys and went back to the cottage to prepare for a walk with Sunny and Jimmy. As we were leaving, I looked into the mobile home to make sure that all was well with the Kong exercise, but I could only see one through the window. That one showed signs of having been chewed, and I came to the conclusion that perhaps the other one had been eaten. Let me explain that I have used Kongs for many years, and they have always remained intact, even against the onslaughts of a young Bull Mastiff. Time then for a phone call to Suzie for advice. She said to wait and see if the pieces of Kong passed naturally through the dog's system.

It did not take very long to find out that Lucy was the guilty party. She continued to pass pieces of red rubber over the course of the next few days, but appeared to suffer no ill effects. Yet another valuable lesson learned.

I had also noticed that Lucy in particular was a scavenger, any little thing that she found outside she would eat, if given the opportunity, and that included small metal objects like nails. That past week then had been one of continued success, providing we discount the Kong episode.

The next Saturday morning I decided to change my routine slightly. I went over and left the mobile home door open, so the two girls could go outside if they so chose to. I went back to the cottage and let Sunny and Jimmy out of the front door…wrong move.

All hell broke loose. Sunny charged out of the cottage garden and spotted Molly just emerging from the mobile home. He immediately ran towards her, Lucy ran as well. It took on the appearance of a disorganised greyhound race. I didn't have a problem with Jimmy, fortunately, as any form of chasing required too much outlay of energy for his liking, he much preferred to stay in just the one spot, alongside me and bark. At that stage there was nothing that I could do but wait, as I knew that Sunny was not chasing Molly in an aggressive manner, he looked upon this as great fun and after a few minutes of dashing about, finally got bored and they all settled down again. I noticed that Lucy appeared to be rather un-nerved by Sunny's behaviour. It was something that I would have to watch out for.

I did not know it at the time, but the heart stopping situations were not to end there. Later on in the afternoon Derek had been into one of the sheds and had inadvertently left the gate open that led into the chicken field. The field covers the best part of an acre, which afforded the poultry a lot of free range. I was not aware that anything untoward had happened and was blissfully working away quite happily with my gardening, thinking all four dogs were in attendance. The next moment, I heard a tremendous clucking and the sound of wings flapping coming from the area around the chicken shed. I turned the corner and was greeted by a veritable snowstorm of chicken feathers. Further inspection showed that Molly and Lucy had gone through the open gate, and the sight of all those chickens must have made them both feel that Christmas had arrived early.

When I got into the chicken field, Lucy was busy chasing the hens in one direction and then the other, but not making any attempt to grab one, or harm them in any way. Unfortunately, the same set of rules did not appear to apply to Molly, who by then had a very firm grip on one of the hens and was busy plucking feathers out of her. The hen was making sufficient noise which served to keep the remainder of the birds further down the field, out of harms way. I shouted at Molly and even before I was able to grab hold of her, she let the hen go and I was then just left with the task of getting her and Lucy back through the gate again. At that stage, from what I had observed, it was obvious that Molly would have continued her attack on the hen if she had not been stopped.

I still could not be sure about Lucy; maybe if she had been given more time she might well have gone on to display the same sort of behaviour to the hen that Molly had done. I was not in a position to know. Anyway, once I had the two of them secured indoors, I returned to the field to check the hen, which by that time had disappeared into the roost and was sitting on the highest perch possible. She was obviously not prepared to put herself forward for that sort of treatment again. I looked over her carefully, but the only damage appeared to be to her feathers, as she had lost several handfuls and they would grow back in time. She seemed none the worse for wear, but I was not going to expect much in the way of eggs from her for the next few days!

For the remainder of that afternoon I put the Dachshunds into the lounge and kept the door shut, just in case of any further slip ups. I did leave the back door open into the kitchen, so that Sunny and Jimmy could follow me in and out. In a way I hoped that Lucy and Molly might follow their lead and venture into the kitchen, but neither of them would even approach the doorway. I tried to throw the odd treat near the threshold, but even that would not entice them any nearer. It was encouraging to note that despite Molly and Sunny being in closer proximity, there were no untoward incidents between them.

On the Sunday morning I went over to let the girls out. Molly appeared to be very uneasy. She would not venture outside the mobile home, which was very unusual. I tried to encourage her out, because I didn't want any more mess inside at that stage and she did, very reluctantly, emerge into the training field but as soon as she spotted Lucy she flew at her and pinned her to the fence.

That was the first time I had ever seen her react in an unfriendly or aggressive manner towards Lucy. I managed to distract her, but I could tell that Lucy was shocked by this behaviour towards her, as I was too. Up until then they had been soulmates, but Molly's whole demeanour appeared to be different somehow and I must confess that I was worried. I could not think of anything that might have unsettled or disturbed her, other than the incident with the hens the day before, but she appeared to have settled down after that and had been fine for the rest of that Saturday. Perhaps she was just feeling a little under the weather…was I trying to read too much into her behaviour? Those alarm bells again.

Mid morning and the sun was shining, hardly a cloud in the sky, just a slight warm north westerly breeze brushing the tops of the long grass.

Yes, ideal conditions for my next job. Time then to cut the grass in the training field. I put the Dachshunds, Sunny and Jimmy, the two sheep, and both goats into one of the secure fields behind the cottage, thus enabling me to leave various gates open between the big field and the training field, to allow me easier access with the motor mower. Lucy and Molly were in the front area by the mobile home, as that was the place that they were used to being free to wander about in.

Just recently the menfolk had carried out a complete check of all the fencing and there was a lot. I had been assured that it was 100 percent secure. I was therefore quite confident that all the livestock and animals were protected and safe, should either Lucy or Molly feel that there might be another opportunity for a chicken supper.

I took the motor mower into the training field and started it up. Equipped with an electric key start, it did make life easier, but I had also been making noises to Derek just recently about how good it would be to have a sit on mower. So far he had not risen to the bait, but who knows, perhaps with a little more gentle persuasion…?

Anyway, I had completed a couple of cuts up and down and was on my way to do the third, when I noticed that Molly had moved from her original spot, where she and Lucy had been dozing in the sun, just outside the training field gate. I wasn't too worried about that because I assumed that she had perhaps got a little too hot in the sun and had gone to lay down in the shade behind the tool shed.

Just as I was commencing my fourth run up the field, I thought that I heard a noise, so I switched off the mower and listened. When working away from the confines of the cottage I am always on the alert if I know Derek is outside, as there were times he was not too stable on his feet, especially if the ground he was on was uneven.

The noise I heard was Derek shouting for me at the top of his voice. At the same time I could hear hens screeching and the noise of dogs obviously in distress. Momentarily I froze; I knew immediately that something was dreadfully wrong. I raced over to the field that I had left the animals contained in and was confronted by the sight of Molly in their midst. Just how in heaven's name had she managed to get into what I had assumed was a totally secure field? Anyway, there she was, trying to attack little Billy, one of the elderly Dachshunds. Sunny, my eldest collie, was blocking her way. I then spotted two dead hens. When I turned again for a closer look at what had taken place, I saw a sight that will live with me forever. There, lying quite still on the ground, was my oldest Dachshund, Solo. I knew immediately that he was dead, and I would never be able to describe my emotions in the few minutes that followed. I was in an absolute rage and confronted Molly, placing myself in a position where I could manoeuvre her with my body towards the nearest gate, which fortunately was just behind her.

Once I had her secured and had closed the gate, I turned again and just stood. I was in a state of total shock. I went over to the spot where Solo was lying and to this present day will never be able to describe the different emotions that overwhelmed me, as I gathered his frail little old body in my arms. I could see straight away that she had bitten him and torn into his side. It had to be borne in mind that he was a long haired dog, so it was possible that she had injured him in other places that I could not see. Solo's back legs were weak, due to his age, and I suspected that she had attacked the weakest first. Billy was also an old dog, but more mobile, so obviously he had been able to try to put space between himself and Molly.

Whatever had I done? I had let that happen to my dear old Solo, my little friend who had joined me in so many activities over the years, from both successes in the show ring, to gaining awards in competitive obedience. He really was such a gentle and loveable soul, and I had allowed his life to end in that way. I was overcome with a variety of different emotions, ranging from guilt, anger and confusion, to absolute and utter despair.

I went indoors and found the nicest blanket I could find to wrap him up in. Why? I do not know, it was all too late now. The damage had been done. I went back to the two dead hens and saw that there was another hen that appeared to have been stripped of a large part of her feathers. In an attempt to make her more comfortable, I placed her in our big outside workshop, under an infra-red lamp and settled her as best as I could. I had to let nature take its natural course, but, despite all my efforts, she died a few hours later. I could find no visible signs of any injury, so assumed that the shock and trauma of her ordeal had been too much for her little system to cope with.

Time then to turn my attention to Molly. She had returned to the mobile home. Lucy meanwhile seemed absolutely oblivious to all that had taken place. When Lucy went back into the mobile home, Molly did not approach her and still seemed to be behaving in an unusual and distant way. They settled down, and I shut them both in and went back to assess the overall damage. Derek was very upset as he had been unable to limit the damage before I could get to the scene of the disturbance. Solo had been a good companion to both of us since he was a puppy and had spent many years with us and our two children, Derek Junior and Suzanne.

I still felt totally numb, it was almost surreal. I made a phone call to the rescue centre and also called Suzie. It was decided by everyone that there was no other alternative but to put Molly to sleep the following morning. I replaced the receiver, and I had to admit that I was unable to do anything at all for a couple of hours. I could not tell you even now what I was thinking about at that time. I was utterly devastated and blamed myself for what had happened. I went all around the fields, examining in close detail all the fencing and despite still looking regularly, even today, I still cannot not see how Molly summoned enough strength to force her way under the chain link fencing, which was tightly secured to the ground at regular intervals. I can only assume that there must have been some small gap, too small for us to notice, but sufficiently large enough for her to squeeze her way through, so great was her determination to get to the hens.

I knew that the fencing had been thoroughly checked and we have never located the point at which she gained entry, and I don't suppose we ever will now. As I went by the mobile home all was very silent. I confess that I did not even look in their direction. It was time then to choose a place to bury our dear old friend Solo. I wanted it to be a very special place that I could go to, in my quieter moments and think of him, not as he was at the end of his life, but to recall the very many hours of love, companionship and faithful friendship that he had given to me during his life. I was unable to see clearly as the tears streamed down my face, I cried and felt sick with guilt and filled with such a great sadness, that I had allowed this old friend's life to come to an untimely end, in such an appalling manner. He was a little dog with such a great heart, an ability that surprised and astounded so many people with his amazing success in competitive obedience when he was young. He was also blessed with a gentle but comical nature that kept us laughing over the years. Having found a suitable place, I buried him in the quiet solitude that our garden afforded and was thankful for those last private moments shared by just the two of us. After a while I went back to the cottage.

Derek and I sat staring into our cups, not speaking, not drinking. Neither of us knew what to say to one another. It came to the time for an evening meal, but once we had fed the dogs, neither of us had an appetite, the thought of food was furthest from our minds.

With many mixed emotions, I made my way over to the mobile home, to feed Lucy and Molly. They both appeared to be in good spirits and were both very eager for their meal. I had to admit that when I saw the anticipation in Molly's expression, as I was preparing her meal, I felt such an overwhelming sadness that her shining light was about to fade. I had never seen a dog with such bright eyes as Molly. They shone like the North Star. My original feelings of anger were replaced by a leaden helpless feeling, knowing what the next day would hold in store for her.

As I let them out into the training field, no one observing their demeanour would have had the vaguest idea what had taken place earlier that day. When I finally settled them down for the night, they just lay quietly.

Later that evening I did a final check, as I usually did, by just peeping through the window, then made my way back to the cottage. Before I even reached the gate I heard Lucy scream, so I crept back and took another guarded look through a gap in the curtains. They were settled again, but this time not together, which was very unusual. Derek and I stayed up late that evening, because I knew that when I did eventually go to bed, sleep was not going to come easily. That assumption proved to be right, as every now and again I could hear Lucy scream. As dawn broke, I could lay there no longer, so I got up, nervous as to what I might find; desperately hoping that Lucy was alright.

When I opened the door of the mobile home they both seemed to be fine, and I was greeted in the usual excited way by both of them. I felt absolutely choked with emotion and could not stop my tears, knowing that it would be the last time I would see Molly like that. She was so happy to see me, and I felt so very angry with myself and an overwhelming sadness for her. They went into the training field, but no sooner did they go through the gate, then Molly pinned Lucy to the fence.

47

Lucy screamed and just as quickly Molly backed off and they were fine again with one another. I then cleaned up a few odds and ends from the mobile home, put it all into a black plastic bag, ready to take over to the bin. Molly came up behind me and attacked the bag. She tore it to shreds. As soon as she grabbed it I let go quickly, as my first thought was that she might then start to attack me. She was in a frenzy, but suddenly stopped and calmly walked away. After a while they returned to the mobile home, and there were no other problems.

Suzie was coming over at lunchtime and she brought Sinead, her veterinary nurse with her to help, should it be necessary. Maureen was coming over from the rescue centre, and she arrived before them. I was so thankful for her company and comfort at that time. Before the others got here, I took the opportunity to shut Lucy into one of the sheds, which was very secure, and a good distance away from the mobile home. I had sedated Molly with a normal dose of Sedalin, which she had taken easily with her food. When Maureen arrived we looked through the window, and Molly was sound asleep on the floor of the lounge. Obviously the sedative had done its job, or so we thought.

A few minutes later Suzie and Sinead arrived, but then, when we looked again, Molly was awake and reacting. I then had to give her more sedative, which thankfully she took with a little food and we stood around outside and waited. It was a grey over-cast day and raining, which really reflected my mood at that time. After a few more minutes I went back inside. Molly was still up and moving about as if she had never had any sedation. I then had to give her more sedative, until I had used up a tube and a half. That would have been enough Sedalin for at least ten dogs. She now appeared to be calm; until Suzie attempted to inject her, she then fought so fiercely that it took the four of us to hold her down, enabling Suzie to euthanize her. During the many years I had owned and worked with dogs, I had been with many when they had been put to rest, but never had one affected me like Molly.

Poor thing, she had only known fear in her life, apart from the relatively short time that she had spent with me and that was the irony of it all. She had just started to gain confidence and to experience some tender and loving care. I wondered if it might be her new found confidence that had enabled her to do what she had done, or was there some other underlying cause that was responsible for her sudden behaviour. Unfortunately, I had not known her for long enough to even hazard a change in guess, and I knew that I would never know the answer.

Suzie, Sinead and Maureen were very kind, and they offered to help me bury her, but I declined, as I had not yet decided as to exactly where I would like her final resting place to be. I wanted to find just the right spot, somewhere with a peaceful aura, to perhaps afford her the peace that she had been unable to find in her young life, but also somewhere away from where my own dogs were buried. This was not because I blamed her in any way for what had happened, but more as a sign of respect for Solo.

Once everyone had gone, I put Lucy back into the mobile home. She seemed very unsettled and very subdued. I put her evening meal down, but she refused to go near it. She sat up on the side that she and Molly had always shared together and just stared at me. I had the feeling that somewhere inside her she was perhaps sharing my sorrow at the day's events and I confess that I could hardly focus on her as the tears streamed down my face. I could not stop crying, I felt so alone, and I sensed that Lucy was feeling the same way too. We sat together for a long time, how long I do not know, both of us silent, but the silence echoing the grief that we both felt.

At that moment I could just not see how I was going to move forward. I hated the thought of Lucy being left on her own. I was worried that the small degree of trust that we had built up might now be destroyed. Would she exhibit different behaviour now that she was on her own? I wondered if her fears might escalate into aggression, having to deal with problems without her partner and companion. Would I be faced with the prospect of having to start at the beginning again? Once again, so many doubts and fears that were unanswerable at that moment in time. I made my way back to the cottage and fed the other dogs. I then prepared myself as best I could to bury Molly.

Earlier in the day I had found a peaceful place beneath some trees. It was a place that I would not have to pass by every day, as I did not want to be constantly reminded of what had happened. I began to dig her grave, but the moment I started, Lucy began to howl. The area I had chosen for Molly was a long way away from the mobile home, completely out of sight and there was no way that Lucy could have seen or known where I was. Her howling continued and it was the most heart rending noise. I had heard nothing like it for well over 30 years and that was when I had seen film footage of a pack of wolves which, at that time, had evoked an interest in their habitat and behaviour. There was no other sound to be heard. It was a still evening and the light was fading. We were surrounded by forestry, and our nearest neighbour was over a half a mile away. I was alone in this quiet place and it made the hairs on my arms stand up. It was an experience that I wished never to be repeated. I was only half way through the digging and but had to stop and go indoors. It was all too much…why had I not accepted the offer of assistance?

I waited ten minutes and went back outside again. It took me a long time to dig a grave large enough, as Molly was quite a big dog. Lucy continued to howl, but I had to finish the task. I gently laid her down. The very moment that I finished covering Molly over with the last spade full of earth and gathered my things together, Lucy stopped howling. The whole situation was eerie and most uncanny because there was no possible way that she could have seen or heard me. Was it just a coincidence? Somehow I do not believe that it was, as I have never heard her doing anything like it again since. I felt wretched as I went indoors and could only keep thinking that I had cost two dogs their lives.

Later that evening I went over to Lucy to let her out before settling her for the night. She was very wary of me and appeared to be unsure of everything again. I had to question what I had done; in trying to do, what at the time, I thought was for the best. It was my opinion that perhaps I had not done so, up to that point, possibly just the opposite. The following morning Lucy was still very subdued, she had shut down again. However, the situation was more settled, as she had ceased barking and lunging at the window, as had happened when she and Molly had been together.

I decided that I would not do very much with Lucy for the rest of that day and give her a chance to settle and adjust to her changed circumstances. The first time she encountered Sunny and Jimmy after the event, she seemed very frightened of Sunny. He snapped at her as she passed him, which he had never done when Molly had been there. Nevertheless I did not have to intervene. She was fine with Jimmy, who was not generally put out by much at all.

# 4

I knew that sooner or later I was going to have to put a slip lead on Lucy, before any further progress could be made. Up to that point Lucy and Molly had gone into a panic at the mere sight of any type of lead, so the prospect did not look at all promising.

The following day was the 1st of May. I started the day by just sitting with her for an hour or so. The fact that I was there, and not expecting her to do anything, had a calming effect on her and she was just enjoying having her chest stroked. Whilst I was doing that, I had tucked a lead close into my side, out of her sight. I had already adjusted the loop so that it was big enough to slip over her, when the right moment presented itself. I had left various leads around the mobile home at different times, so she was familiar with the sight of them. I then tried to establish the right moment to slip the lead over her neck, but the moment I managed to do that she went berserk. Unfortunately, in her efforts to extricate herself from the lead, she only succeeded in managing to tighten it.

Past experience with Lucy had taught me that it was best just to sit quietly, as if nothing had happened. I knew she would tire, so I waited until she was in a corner and approached her calmly. She let me know in no uncertain terms that she wanted me to back off. On that occasion, I had to take the chance that she wouldn't back up her vocal threat in a more physical manner. It was necessary for me to remove the slip lead before she caused herself an injury. I took hold of the lead and fortunately she just froze. I quickly removed the lead and left it on the floor. I returned to my seat and acted as if nothing had happened. Lucy sat motionless and just stared at me. I stayed for a few minutes and decided that it might be best to leave her to her own devices for a little while.

What had just occurred in that episode had taught me that the only way I was ever going to get a lead on Lucy safely, would be to sedate her very slightly. Once she had a collar on, it would then be a more simple matter to clip a lead on, as opposed to trying to slip a lead over her head. I did, however, leave it for a few days before proceeding with the lead project and decided to concentrate instead on trying to introduce her to the cottage. She had already had experience of running around in our very large front garden, which probably extends to over half an acre, so she was already familiar with everything outside. Going into the cottage was going to be a different matter, so I just left the front door open, but at that stage did not attempt to encourage her inside. She did eventually step over the threshold, on to the mat inside the front door, and I did notice that she was not so frightened of Sunny now. He did ignore her for the majority of the time, which in itself was a blessing.

On May 6th, which was a Saturday, she came into the lounge for the first time. She settled down on the rug in front of the fire. I had allowed no other dogs into the room for obvious reasons. I had at that point decided to sedate her mildly, in order to put the collar on. I did it without too much difficulty, but when she realised she had it on, she shut down again.

I had expected her to paw at the collar and rub her neck, but she just remained very quiet. She refused to look at me, nor would she let me go near her.

I felt that it was about time to have another talk with Suzie; perhaps with the possibility of putting Lucy on a mild tranquiliser to allow me to work with her and help her overcome her worst fears. I didn't really want to do that, but time was passing and each day I was becoming more and more concerned. To enable me to go further with introducing Lucy to so many different situations, the lead was going to be most necessary. Fortunately, by the fifth day she did seem to be a little more relaxed, and at that point we slowly regained a form of communication. I took things very slowly for the next couple of weeks, attempting nothing else that was unfamiliar, so we did make a little progress in the right direction. I was ever mindful that the episode with the slip lead had proved to me, once and for all, how fragile our relationship was.

After two weeks, I decided that she was calm enough for me to try to put a lead on her. Enough time had elapsed since she had been introduced to the collar, so I waited for her until she was relaxed beside me and then very quickly clipped the lead onto her collar. In a manner of speaking that really did put the cat among the pigeons. She went wild and started to try and walk the walls of the mobile home. I stood back and gave her a few minutes to calm down, but I could see calming down was not going to happen. I did manage to steady her in one corner and speedily removed the lead. As I did that she grabbed my forearm with both her front legs and the grip that she possessed was unbelievable. She was very still and although I did avoid making eye contact with her, I just knew that she had me fixed with her unblinking stare. I must admit that it made me feel very nervous, as I had no vague idea as to what would come next. She continued to maintain her vice like grip on my arm and that was proving to be rather painful. She made no attempt to release me, just continued to grip. I happened to be able to see the clock, so I endeavoured to focus on the passing of time, to take my attention away from the discomfort I was feeling in my arm. I timed the incident, which lasted for over three minutes. That doesn't sound very long, but believe me it was an unpleasant three minutes in that situation.

Eventually she did relax her grip, but I decided not to move straight away. I sat back down on the seat by the window and reached for a book. I opened it and scanned the pages, not really reading anything, just feeling concern for the whole episode. In all my years of experience with dogs of all ages and breeds, I had never come across that type of behaviour before. I was then left with some more questions that would have to be answered and further problems that would have to be addressed. I stayed with her for another ten minutes and then returned to the cottage. I sat in the kitchen nursing a cup of tea, reflecting on what had just taken place and what should come next. I knew that Derek was upstairs on the computer and I wondered what he was going to say when I told him what had happened. I did not disturb him; I felt it better to tell him when he was not being distracted by the internet.

Over the course of the next few days I left the lead around, picking it up and putting it down near her, showing her that I had no intention of doing anything with the lead as far as she was concerned. I made no attempt to approach her with it, but even her reaction to its presence confirmed my fears that I was not going to succeed in putting it on her, at that stage, only with a tremendous struggle.

As luck and good fortune would have it, the next weekend provided the ideal opportunity to make some progress. I had no lessons booked in for the Saturday and was not expecting any visitors. Time now to take the bull by the horns, or better still, the dog by the collar and let us get that lead on for once and for all. Now, positive thinking was demanded. The plan involved getting the lead on, come what may, and then leading her to the training field. Once that had been accomplished, after all I was the trainer, things should not be too difficult. I approached the mobile home filled with a mixture of anticipation, determination and sheer dread. I did wonder if pushing her to a new limit would trigger another leg or arm gripping episode, once she realised that she was being restricted in that manner. Anyway, in through the door, no hesitation, straight up to Lucy, took hold of her collar and clipped the lead on.

She went crazy. She leapt about, screamed and did back flips and somersaults, as I tried to move towards the door. Before reaching the door I was perspiring quite freely, and I hadn't even got to the field then.

As we went down the steps she almost took me off my feet with her gyrations, and I had a difficult job in restraining her once we were outside. The field was only a few yards away but the resistance, coupled with her strength, was really quite phenomenal, for a dog of her stature.

We made it to the field and I just stood sideways to her and she did the same. I made no attempt at eye contact but I could tell that she was staring at me, no doubt waiting to see what the next move would be. We stayed that way for about 15 minutes, neither of us moving. This gave me the chance to cool down and regain my composure, after my previous exertions.

I resumed by moving one of my feet slightly and she immediately responded by lunging and leaping two feet or more in the air. I stood still again but any movement that I made, however small, was met with the same response from Lucy. I had to accept that if progress was to be made then I just had to persevere with the initial exercise, until such time as she was able to accept being on the lead. So, slowly and gradually I increased my movements, until I reached the point where I was able to move a couple of paces. Her objections were now limited to leaping up and trying to grab the lead between her paws, in much the same

way as she had displayed her grabbing technique with my arm
and leg previously. I sensed that her behaviour was more to do
with her being of a determined nature, as opposed to being
frightened. Two could play at that game, I thought, because for
my part I was just as determined, if not more so, to keep on going,
until the time came when we could at least walk a few steps,
without her objecting.

At last, four and then five steps were taken without any protest.
Yes… success at last. It had taken just over six hours to reach this
point, and I don't know how Lucy felt but I was exhausted and
almost close to tears. Even at that late stage her strength had never
waned, not for one single moment in the day.

Her constant pulling on the lead had given me a pain in the
shoulder. I must admit that I felt like just having done a couple
of rounds with Mike Tyson and come off the loser. Anyway, as
soon as we had completed four steps, I immediately took the lead
off and went back to the mobile home. Lucy seemed to be
unperturbed by the days strenuous events and followed me
inside. I did notice that she was thoroughly relaxed, unlike me. I
was so tired it took an effort just to place one foot in front of the
other. I gave Lucy her tea and then went over to the cottage to
feed the rest of the dogs and join Derek for the evening meal.

I should mention at that point that although Derek is
disabled, he does do a lot of the small jobs around the cottage,
whilst I am engaged with the business, and I am thankful that
one of these 'little jobs" is doing the cooking. I have to tell you
that I can cook when the need arises, but by the time I have
finished, there is hardly a pan left unused. Worktop space no

longer exists and the kitchen looks like the aftermath of five celebrity chefs. I never cease to wonder how he can serve up the meal, and when I look around there is hardly a dirty utensil in sight. The working surfaces are the same as when he started. I know I should take note, but then I might get coerced into doing some of the cooking, and that would never do. After the meal and a couple of glasses of homemade red wine, another of Derek's little saving graces, I felt fine again.

I decided to take Sunny and Jimmy out for a long evening walk. It was probably the effect of the extra glass of wine that then prompted the thought, 'why not take Lucy along as well?'

When I ran the idea by Derek, he said that he felt I might have had enough for one day, but the wine had given me Dutch courage. I let Sunny and Jimmy out into the garden and went over to collect Lucy.

No doubt she had already considered the day to be over as far as further exercise was concerned, so she appeared a little wary when I made my entrance again. I had to corner her again to get the lead on, but without hesitation, walked outside with her. I took no notice of the lunging and leaping about, her antics soon ceased and she walked with me. I must confess that I had expected a more prolonged protest.

Once we had gone past the front gates of the cottage and entered unfamiliar ground, she became extremely agitated. Progress on the walk was a lot slower than it usually was, but despite the reduced pace Sunny and Jimmy took no notice of her. I was able to keep Sunny occupied by throwing his ball, and Jimmy was obviously very pleased to be going at such a leisurely pace – not a great one for strenuous exertion is Jimmy.

We had only gone a few yards when we came across fox droppings. Nothing unusual in that, because where we live we are surrounded by bog land, forestry, fields and distant farms, which made the whole area an ideal hunting ground for the foxes, badgers and the occasional mink. As I have said before we have many kinds of birds, ranging from the tiny wren to the very much larger heron and all other sizes in between. We do not have a cat; poor thing wouldn't stand a chance with our doggie family, so our wildlife friends have it all to themselves. Occasionally a kestrel might swoop down and capture an unsuspecting fledgling, but other than that there are no predators.

Well, back to the fox episode. Lucy reacted in a fearful way, either to the scent of the fox or the droppings. That surprised me as I had expected no reaction, other than perhaps her wanting to eat the droppings or roll in it… she seemed terrified. It was not a one off reaction, as we came across fox signs in four other places on the walk, and Lucy behaved in exactly the same way as she had done on the first occasion.

The surprises were not over yet. We do have a cuckoo, who is a regular spring visitor and at that time of the year it was looking out for a nest to take over, when it started to cry, Lucy displayed signs of extreme agitation and seemed very disturbed by the noise.

Thankfully, the remainder of the walk was uneventful. Lucy calmed down, provided I kept walking, but did tend to show signs of panic if I were to slow down or pause. At that stage, even though it was at the end of what had been an incredibly long and tiring day, I felt elation at the fact that Lucy and I had taken a huge step forward, in further cementing our hitherto tenuous relationship. Maybe we were then approaching the stage where I would be able to introduce her to other new experiences?

Over the course of the next few days I concentrated, when I could, in giving her plenty of walking practice. She was now walking nicely on the lead and never made any attempt to pull ahead of me. She was still showing signs of panic when she heard the cuckoo, who was always most audible early in the day, but she no longer showed any reaction to the fox droppings. She looked at me constantly during our walks and still did not like it if we had to stop for any reason. She did not appear to be bothered by Sunny and Jimmy running around, back and forth. Sometimes Sunny would come right up to her, and she would then immediately lower her body, tuck her tail in and look away. Jimmy rarely acknowledged her, but then again he doesn't take too much notice of the rest of the pack, so nothing unusual there then.

When she finally seemed to be comfortable on the lead, I was curious to know what her response would be to a moving vehicle, so I started our car, left the engine running and walked Lucy past it a couple of times. It seemed to make no impression on her, neither good nor bad.

She was then at the stage where she was spending short periods of time inside the cottage, but she made very sure that the doors were always left open. Providing she could see an escape route, she then had nothing to worry about. Had that option not been available, I know that she would have panicked.

As we were approaching the end of May, I felt it was time to try shutting one of the doors of the cottage. I waited for her to settle down in the lounge, in her usual place on the rug by the fire and then went and quietly closed the back door, knowing that she could only see the front door from where she was laying. All went well and she was not aware that I had done anything out of the ordinary. I think that she may have sensed that something was going on, but could not quite make out what.

One thing was noticeable however and that was as soon as any of the other dogs ventured into the front room, she left immediately. On one or two occasions previously she had taken to lying on the stairs, in the dark, where the staircase turns at right angles to the upstairs landing. That enabled her to be aware of who came and went by any of the downstairs doors, and she would also have ample warning if anyone approached the stairs to use the upstairs toilet. All in all a very good vantage point. I was happy that she had found a situation that she was comfortable with where she did not feel threatened. I was not concerned about her adopting it as a safe haven, even though it meant someone having to pass her occasionally, as she had never shown any signs of assertive behaviour, either with us, or the other dogs.

# 5

---

In due course she eventually became used to being in the cottage with all the doors shut and no longer appeared to be disturbed by movement from the other household occupants. I then felt that it was time for Lucy to take her place with us, on a permanent basis in the cottage. She had been in her own little domain long enough and should be ready to take another step towards rehabilitation and normality.

I decided that before that could happen, Lucy should have a bath. I anticipated that perhaps that might be easier said than done, so I enlisted Derek's help, thinking that two pairs of hands would be better than one.

It was a lovely warm sunny day, so I held her on her lead just by the back door of the cottage, used plenty of doggie shampoo and washed her off with buckets of warm water, which we passed from one to the other, relay fashion. It was obvious that Lucy was not welcoming such treatment, as I knew that she had never been subjected to an experience like that before in the awful place that she had been kept in. She made no protest, but did give me the impression that she might snap as I was washing her tail. She certainly did not like the sensation of being dried off with the towels, again something that she was not used to, as it meant having something wrapped around her. Once she was dry, what a difference there was in her appearance. She was truly a totally different colour, and the doggie smells had all gone. The shampoo and washing had produced masses of hair on the ground, leaving her coat clean and shining.

I had chosen to bath Lucy outside, as opposed to using the shower unit in the mobile home, as that would have meant her being enclosed in a very small space, which would undoubtedly have unsettled her again. The mobile home had been her home for quite a while, and I therefore did not want her to associate being in there with an unpleasant experience. We still had a long way to go in our relationship, and at that stage I did not want to rule out the option of being able to use the mobile home on the odd occasion that it might prove necessary.

We then decided to invest in a hot and cold outside shower, which could be used for all the dogs, which would be much more pleasant for them all, especially when the colder weather came along. It also made life easier for us, as it would do away with the buckets passing back and forth and something that I could manage on my own, should Derek be unable to assist.

Anyway, after their tea Lucy stayed in the cottage. She settled in her favourite place on the stair by the landing and was as good as gold. I had put a blanket down for her but she tossed it aside, obviously preferring the carpet.

I was happy that she was away from the mobile home because she was becoming territorial and of course it had become her secure retreat.

The following morning Lucy went into the garden happily enough. The other dogs took no notice of her. However, getting her back again into the cottage was a different matter altogether. We finally ended up by leaving the front door open, made sure no one was around and that all the other dogs were shut in the kitchen. She did come in but only as far as the front doormat, but as soon as I opened the kitchen door, she disappeared outside again. After a while she did decide to honour us with her presence and took up her place once again on the landing, where she slept.

That was then to become her resting and sleeping place for the future, in the cottage. It took a further five weeks before she would come into the cottage when someone else was there. The door always had to remain open. We spent a few chilly weeks waiting and shivering, until she eventually progressed to coming into the lounge. If no one was around she would settle in front of the fire. As soon as the other dogs, or Derek and I appeared, she was gone. Even today she will venture into the lounge when we are all sitting for the evening and she will walk around, perhaps tolerate a little fussing from one of us, but then be gone as quickly as she came, back once more to her landing. She disliked coming into the kitchen even more and still gets very agitated when she wanders in and the door is closed behind her. If I do need to contain her in the kitchen for any reason, she will pace back and forth until she can leave.

The first time that she had to be left for any length of time was when Derek and I had an appointment in Sligo town, which is about 24 miles from where we live. We were going to be gone for quite some time, so I decided to leave her in her usual place, on the landing, where she settled. Sunny and Jimmy always stayed in the lounge. At that stage I did not know how she would cope with being left like that.

Whilst we were out I had visions in my mind of Bedlam. If she panicked, would Sunny then react? He had never tolerated excitable dogs and was always very quick to put them in their place.

Jimmy, on the other hand, never seemed to know quite what to do, so that if he was in doubt, he dealt with the situation by resorting to a high pitched repetitive whine. That was guaranteed to make matters infinitely worse. Thus, my morning coffee with Derek in our favourite café, was marred by a mental video of utter chaos and mayhem taking place in my absence. I was aware that he was talking to me, and on a couple of occasions he asked me if I was listening to anything he said. I had to give him short answer… NO.

By the time we got to cottage gate, I had done a good job of convincing myself that the very worst of all my fears were about to come true. I got out of the car and listened, but there was no noise. As I opened the gate Jimmy barked. I unlocked the door and let Sunny and Jimmy out. I looked up the stairs, and it appeared that Lucy had not moved. She would not come down, so Derek went into the kitchen and I then went up the stairs and got behind her. She didn't like the idea of that and raced down the stairs and out the front door. I had a quick check around, and everything appeared to be normal. No chewed woodwork or shredded carpet could be seen, so I was then able to breathe a sigh of relief that nothing untoward had taken place in our absence.

At the end of the month I decided to let Lucy off the lead during our morning walk across the bog land. She started to venture too far out for my liking, so I sent Sunny off to bring her in, which he did without too much fuss. She kept with us then for the remainder of the walk, until we returned to the cottage.

I realised that I had taken a huge risk really, by letting her loose, but I somehow sensed that she was ready. She did appear to be somewhat unsettled when we eventually got back and then, later in the day, when I was in the training field with her, without any warning, she suddenly gripped the top of my leg with her front legs. That was exactly the same behaviour that she had displayed previously in the episode with my arm. She was just staring at me, and the pressure that she was able to exert by her two legged grip was hurting my leg. I looked away from her and tried to keep my body relaxed, despite feeling a little uneasy, to say the very least, but she gave no indication of wanting to let go.

I wondered could we perhaps negotiate, but then maybe not. Actually I was quite pleased that there was no one else around at that time, as I was beginning to feel rather silly standing in the middle of a field, with a dog wrapped around one leg. She continued her grip for another three minutes or so, and then let go and wandered off. I avoided looking at her but didn't leave the training field. Instead, I walked around slowly for a few minutes, then headed back towards the cottage. Lucy followed me and there were no further incidents that day. She had however managed to leave an almost circular bruise around my leg.

When I spoke to Suzie about the incident and showed her the bruise, she did ask me if I was still sure that I was doing the right thing. I readily admit that I was not 100 per cent sure, but really was as sure as I could have been, given the uncertainty of everything that had happened so far with her. There was no similarity to any domestic dog that I had ever encountered in my life. I knew I was making mistakes. She did let me know that in no uncertain terms, but the knowledge I was gaining was invaluable.

Lucy was becoming stronger and stronger each day and would attempt to run a little at times, but only for a few paces. I was fortunate to witness a most amusing incident one afternoon, whilst working in the garden. Lucy tried to entice Jimmy into playing, but he looked terrified and went and hid under a bush. Not only that, but it took him quite some time to work out that it was safe to emerge.

It was also at that time I decided to introduce her to my elderly miniature Dachshunds. I was very nervous as I could not imagine how she would perceive them. Would she be able to accommodate their presence, or would they perhaps appear to pose a threat to her, I had no way of knowing. I could not help but look back at what had happened with Solo, and from past experience knew just how quickly a dog could attack. Secured in the small enclosed area at the rear of the cottage, I felt that it would be the safest place to make all the initial introductions. Derek was sitting at the patio table, and the little ones were enjoying basking in the warmth of the sun. I allowed Lucy to come in via the side gate, but left it open for her to have an escape route, should she feel overwhelmed and also somewhere I could get her out quickly, if the need arose. She came in and as soon as she spotted the Dachshunds, she tensed.

Archie, the eldest, went straight up to her, whilst I stood ready to intervene if necessary. Lucy was not happy at his bold behaviour, and she stiffened and curled her lip up. I called Archie, but unfortunately he suffered from selective deafness and as usual, totally ignored me. He was extremely frail, and his eyesight was poor, so I felt it wise to step between them. Carrie was also elderly and not in good health. She had an auto immune problem and had only one kidney. Her joints would swell and that in turn limited her movements. Billy was keeping a safe distance at all times. Last but not least came Jack, who was old, but in good health, apart from being genuinely a little deaf. Altogether the four of them were very vulnerable, and as I have stressed before, I was very aware as to how quickly Lucy could attack, if she so chose.

Carrie and Jack were curious and made an attempt to approach Lucy, but her body language obviously made it clear to them that she wanted them to stay away. Both of them turned tail at the same time. Archie, however, persisted in going up to her, despite my attempts at blocking him from so doing. Each time she tried to let him know in a very positive way that he was not welcome. His vision was very restricted, and I guess he was oblivious to the signals she was trying to give him, so I picked him up and put him out of harm's way. Lucy then started to pace once more, despite the fact that she could have gone out of the back gate again and away from the situation.

She made no attempt to approach Carrie or Jack, but it was apparent that she was disturbed by the first meeting. I have to say at that point that she wasn't the only one. I remained on the alert and ready to take action if necessary. We stayed outside for about 30 minutes or so, but when it became clear that Lucy was not going to settle and relax with the little dogs there, I took them into the cottage. Once they were inside and the door was shut, Lucy ceased pacing and settled down in the shade of one of the bushes. Sunny and Jimmy both walked past her, and she took no notice of either of them. I was hoping that her behaviour that afternoon was occasioned by the fact that it was the first time that she had seen the little dogs.

I did hope it was not because she disliked them in some way, or that perhaps they had triggered a memory from her past. I had been told that there were dead animals where Lucy and the others had been found. Up until then I had always kept the Dachshunds in a separate room, away from Lucy, but that was not an arrangement that we liked or wished to continue. So the following day I decided to introduce the little ones again, but then I let them into the front garden. There are lots of trees and different pathways, in a way, a little like an untidy maze.

I left Jimmy inside the cottage, because if anything

untoward should happen he would be bound to start his painful singing, which would help no one. I knew that if Lucy attempted to chase any of the little ones, or they cried, then Sunny would intervene immediately, so I let him accompany us.

I did some weeding, moving from place to place, at the same time keeping a watchful eye open for Jack and Carrie. They were both slow in their movements, but it was a lovely day, with clear blue skies, so they were very content to just lie out and enjoy the warmth of the sun. Not the case with old Archie. He was again determined to make contact with Lucy. I kept Sunny with me and moved slowly towards Lucy. She did nothing other than to turn her head away and tuck her tail under…she was frightened of him. I continued to watch them carefully and Archie, being so much smaller, managed to sniff her back leg. She remained motionless throughout.

Thankfully that short sniff seemed to satisfy his curiosity, and he walked away. She remained in the same position for a few moments and then disappeared behind the trees, where she remained for the rest of the afternoon, until it was time for everyone to come in.

During the next few days I let them out together in different areas, and on those occasions they totally ignored each other. Lucy would not pass by any of the other dogs, and if one of them walked in her direction she vanished. I decided it might be a good time to see their reaction to one another inside the cottage. That evening we left the kitchen door open. Archie, Billy, Jack, and Carrie came into the lounge, but Lucy was not at all comfortable with the situation. She proceeded to pace up and down the stairs. When I let Sunny and Jimmy into the garden, halfway through the evening, she would normally have gone out with them, but this time she remained upstairs. She did relax however, once I had put the little ones to bed for the evening.

During the course of the next few weeks, Lucy gradually accepted their presence, but even to this day she has never made any attempt at any real contact with them. She still hates it if Archie approaches her and neither Jack nor Carrie have ever attempted to, since their first rebuff. Should they come in any way close to her then she still disappears to her place at the top of the stairs.

June arrived and with it new growth appeared on all the bushes and plants, the roses were in bloom and there must have been a thousand and one bulbs adding random splashes of welcome colour in amongst the greenery. Winter always seemed so long, with its short dark days and overcast and rainy skies. At that stage Lucy was coming in through the back door of the kitchen, even whilst the Dachshunds were there. She was good when we went for a walk and always came back to me immediately, even when something might have distracted her. She constantly looked back at me, to make sure that I was still there and that she continued to do every few seconds.

Over the previous weeks since Lucy had been living in the cottage, we had different friends visit us in the evening for a meal, drinks and some social chit chat.

During those times Lucy would remain on the stairs and greet all and sundry with a continuous growl. Our guests would already have been warned not to make eye contact with her or acknowledge her in any way. Once visitors were settled in the lounge she quietened down, but as soon as anyone moved from the lounge to the kitchen, she would react by growling again. She always kept her distance, either at the top of the stairs, or on the landing, so it presented no problem to our friends. She did not like young children, so I therefore had to ensure that she was kept in another room, on the rare occasions that we did have children visiting.

I started to introduce her to other people and their dogs when they came for lessons. I always chose dogs that were non reactive. In every instance she was frightened of the dogs, and she froze if they approached her. Her behaviour did not surprise me because Maureen had told me previously that she had seen members of Lucy's pack pin her against the wall at her old home, if you could call it that, on several occasions.

She was not so wary of the owners and would take a treat from someone holding out their hand, but she would stretch her neck out to its fullest extent in order to keep as much distance between her and them as was possible.

Around about that time, after some in house discussion, we decided that it might be a good idea to hold a Fun Day Dog Show. A provisional date was pencilled in for the beginning of September. Historically, September had always seemed to be a settled month with a good proportion of sunny days, so we felt that we might just be lucky. We knew that it would take a few weeks to organise. Derek would take care of the administration side of things and design all the posters, event schedules, entry forms and so on. I was the first to admit that I was completely useless at doing anything like that.

Name badges were a priority, as it would be by invitation only and not open to the general public, only to people who had come to me with their dogs for training. It would be my job to send out the invitations, organise the various stalls, decide what classes to hold and just about one hundred and one other jobs that would need to be done before the big day. I was beginning to see that what had started out as a small nucleus of an idea over the breakfast table, was now evolving into a major event. Derek and I worked away each day, when we could and slowly but surely it all started to come together.

I wanted to start obedience training with Lucy, but although she followed me into the training shed she immediately went into a corner and just stared at me. I put some relaxing music on, sat and did some paperwork and ignored her. I had treats with me which I put on the table. I made a cup of coffee and resigned myself to the fact that this would be the extent of our intended training session. However, Lucy did enjoy treats and I had chicken with me. After about ten minutes her sense of smell got the better of her doubts, and she came over to me, with her nose up, sniffing the chicken. I continued to ignore her. I finished my tea and stood up to put my cup back on the side. She immediately went back to her corner. I decided to leave it at that for our first visit to the training shed. When I gathered my things together and opened the door, Lucy remained in the corner. I took a piece of chicken out of the bag approach me, albeit cautiously and took the treat from my outstretched hand.

The following day I took her over to the shed again and repeated the same routine. She adopted her position in the same corner and again, after a few minutes, came over, having sniffed the chicken. This time I asked her to sit, which I had taught her to do in the early days. She did so immediately, so I gave her a handful of chicken. I could see she was keen, and it was very tempting to try to progress further, but I knew that I had to approach any attempt at training with great caution, so I picked up my things and left the training shed.

I went through this same routine for a week and then progressed from asking her to sit, whilst I was still sitting at the table, to then standing up. She stepped aside with her tail tucked under, so I went back a step and sat back down. She then sat immediately. I then knelt down, turned sideways to her and asked her to sit. She did so. I continued to repeat this for another two days and then tried standing, keeping my body sideways to her. She did not like me near her in an upright position. I kept going back a step, and it took a total of ten days for her to feel confident enough to sit when I asked her to, whilst I was in a standing position, although I still could not face her I had to admit that I was pleased with the progress. I have endless patience, and I would definitely have to draw on that in the months to come.

I kept repeating the same actions in different locations, once I was sure that she was confident and relaxed, I then tried facing her. She was fine, so another step forward.

During the month I taught her all the basic commands. I found it quite tiring because the slightest wrong move on my part or using the wrong tone of voice, would result in her shutting down, and that would be the end of any attempt to try to do anything at all with her for the rest of that day. Lucy could not cope with any change in her routine at that time. If anything, however small or unfamiliar occurred, she would start to pace. She would not settle at all. I could never seem to reach her at those times. It was as if we had made no progress whatsoever over the previous months. I just had to wait, perhaps for a day or two, for her to become calm before I could attempt to communicate with her again. It was quite a frustrating time and one thing had been made very clear to me. I could not tell Lucy to do anything, I had to ask her. This is a philosophy I usually apply when training a bitch, but none have ever brought it home to me in the way that Lucy did. I always feel pleased when any dog wants to do something for me, but with Lucy I felt privileged that she would even consider working with me. At that stage our relationship was tenuous, and I knew it would take a long time for the relationship to gain strength and to discover a friendship that I hoped, one day, to earn.

Lucy before the rescue.

The place where they were found.

Molly and Lucy in the mobile home.

Lucy's first visit with Suzie.

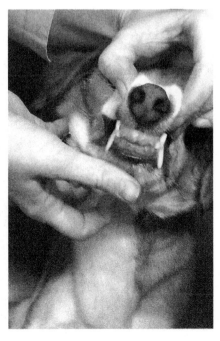

Lucy's front teeth, worn down.

Lucy waking from her operation.

Resting after her operation.

Lucy and Jimmy.

Lucy friends with Sunny during her season.

Strutting our stuff at the show.

Smile please!

**Derek and Lucy share a moment.**

**With Maureen… friends now.**

# 6

Our close friends Madge and Don came to stay with us for a week. They have been our friends for over 30 years. They lived near us in England and were used to sharing our company with a variety of different dogs. When they first came into the cottage Lucy growled and paced up and down and would not go into any room, if they were there. They totally ignored her. She would not acknowledge them at all during that week, until the day that they were leaving. They were standing in the hallway, and Lucy came down the stairs. Madge put out her hand and Lucy sniffed it before disappearing back upstairs again, but she didn't growl. All a bit late as they were leaving, but had they been staying for a few extra days she might well have accepted their presence.

The following week I tried to introduce Lucy to a couple who were training their dogs with me. I brought her over to them in the training field. She was not happy. She was very frightened of their dogs, and although I kept my distance with her and tried to keep her focus on me with her favourite treat of chicken, she just crouched down, tail between her legs, ears back. I don't think that she was even aware of me, or the food I offered. As soon as she showed this degree of distress, I calmly walked her away. I took her back to the cottage and then went to say goodbye to the folks and their dogs. When I returned to the cottage, Lucy did her usual thing when anything untoward happened and totally ignored me. She would not come anywhere near me.

I had chosen very non-reactive relaxed dogs for this introduction, but this had shown me I would have to think very carefully before I attempted to introduce unknown dogs to her in future.

To end the month of June another event took place, which I am sure added a few more grey hairs to what seemed like an already alarming number. I was cleaning out the duck shed after feeding them. The dogs were in the front garden. I finished the shed and then made my way to the next field to fill the goats water container. In the meantime Derek was upstairs in the computer room, which overlooks the duck pond. Unbeknown to me, I had not bolted the gate properly that led into the duck compound. Lucy soon discovered that.

Derek said that when he first spotted her he was very concerned but quickly realised that she was taking no notice of the ducks at all, but more interested in eating any remaining pellets she could find. She also found a couple of duck eggs that I had missed on my morning round. He kept a watchful eye on her and then he heard me come in through the back door. He shouted down to me that Lucy was in the duck field, but I didn't give him chance to tell me that she was doing no harm. I was out through the back door like a shot, possibly the fastest that I had moved for years.

When I got to the duck enclosure I couldn't see Lucy, but the ducks were all calm. They were used to Sunny, Jimmy and the dachshunds, as they had never show any interest in the ducks. I called out to Lucy but she did not respond, and then I heard a noise coming from the duck shed, so I bent down and looked in through the pop hole and got showered in shavings! Lucy was digging frantically with her front paws, sending the shavings towards the entrance with great force. I had to step back as I caught it full in my face. When I could focus again, I went to the front of the shed and opened the main door to discover that she had completely wrecked the nesting area, so I assumed that she had been searching for eggs. She had also managed to tear into one of the new 40kg bales of new shavings, and she was then barely visible in the dust cloud that she had created.

She totally ignored me so I left her to it. I stayed in the duck field, and eventually she emerged. When she saw me, she shot back through the side gate into the front garden. I knew that she was not interested in the ducks or the hens, which was a great relief.

We were now in the month of July, and Lucy was showing signs of coming into season. All my dogs are castrated so I was not bothered, although a little concerned about letting her off her lead over the bogland. We rarely saw a stray dog, but I did wonder if she might be tempted to venture somewhere herself. She was flirting with Sunny, and at that time their bond definitely became stronger. They even slept close to one another on several occasions.

During her season she seemed to be more relaxed, and I was sure this time had helped a great deal in establishing her relationship within the pack. I enjoy Heelwork to Music and have had so much pleasure working with Jimmy, teaching him lots of different moves and then working out a routine using these moves which is in rhythm to a piece of music. It helps form a really close bond with a dog and is great fun, as well as good exercise and teaches a dog self control and the ability to focus.

I was hoping to be able to work with Lucy in that way, now that she knew the basic obedience commands. For the first attempt I chose a short piece of music and just played it whilst working with her doing basic obedience, just to get her used to loud music in the background. I then progressed to teaching her very simple moves, and she seemed to enjoy doing something different, especially as she got a nice treat for doing it. I kept the sessions very short, no more than five minutes at a time. However I still had to be careful with my movements because she would suddenly go into a corner of the shed and shut down. Very often I was not aware as to what I had done to cause this response. I have always found working with a dog in that way to be a great help in building their confidence and felt it was certainly helping Lucy.

Since she had been living in the cottage, we had friends visiting us a usual and Lucy had not been very happy on those occasions. She would growl and pace around upstairs at the slightest movement from anyone. Everyone knew that she had to be ignored and that no one should make eye contact with her. She was always unsettled the following day.

I had learned not to attempt to do anything with her at those times. It was when she appeared to be uneasy that she would attempt to grab my leg or arm with her front legs. I was very aware of her moods and tried to avoid giving her any opportunity to do that. If I sat on the settee Lucy would occasionally come and sit next to me, but I could not look towards her or move an inch because she would be gone. During the last week of July, Maria Lahiff, co-ordinator of the Garda Diversion Project known as Youth Action Project Sligo (YAPS), brought two lads who had shown a particular interest in the dogs. Maria did a marvelous job re-educating and teaching those in her care, the importance of treating all animals with kindness and respect.

They had visited me before as part of a larger group of young people, but these two lads were very keen to work with Jimmy. He was more than happy to oblige, as he was always willing to show off his dancing skills. I brought Lucy out, and when I took her into the training field she barked and growled when she saw the visitors. I had already discussed with them the need to ignore Lucy and they knew her history from their previous visits. I distracted her and encouraged her to work with me which she did, whilst keeping a close eye on everybody else at the same time!

Once she was more relaxed I approached Maria and the boys with her, and she accepted treats from them. I was very pleased with her reaction. This visit was the point that I recognized just what progress we had made. It gave me an opportunity to stand back and observe Lucy with other people. It gave me great encouragement.

August had arrived and my main focus then was working with Lucy, together with Jimmy, in preparation for the show. I was hoping that I could put together a short routine working with both of them. Nothing like being the supreme optimist. Lucy really enjoyed doing the different moves, so it was not difficult teaching her basic ones, such as 'twist' and weaving through my legs, also keeping close to me whichever way I turned. The one thing that took me completely by surprise was when I attempted to teach her to bow. I reached under her and very gently went to hold her tummy up to stop her lying flat and she screamed and screeched. This was quite a setback because she was very reluctant to come into the training shed the following day, and it took a further eight days before she was willing to work with me again. Yet another reminder of how careful I had to be. Just when I thought we had reached another milestone, she always managed to bring me back to earth.

I started off slowly again and just did very short sessions, much to Jimmy's dismay as he would have worked all day long. He loved the Heelwork to Music and would often show off his moves, if he was bored, when I was perhaps talking to someone.

I knew Lucy was really keen the day I opened the cottage gate, and she raced across to the training shed before me and stood waiting for me to open the door. She has done this ever since.

We had friends staying for a few days, and Lucy was not at all relaxed during that time. She would not approach them, and it unsettled her enough for it to disrupt the training programme once again and each day was a day nearer the show! During the week I actually decided not to attempt to do anything with her at the show. I just did not think that I would have time to prepare for the event, which was only fourteen days away.

However, when we were back in our normal routine she settled very quickly, and I was then able to pick up where I had left off with her training. In fact she seemed to be very keen, and I was then given the opportunity to work out a very simple routine to 'Good Golly Miss Molly' by Little Richard, which was a very short but lively piece of music.

Both her and Jimmy were enjoying doing that so much, I was then able to practice a lot, doing very short sessions at different times of the day. Lucy would often make up her own moves as we were all working together. She looked so funny because she would always open her mouth in what appeared to be a laugh when she was excited. This gave her a very comical look because she only had her canine teeth showing. It was such a great reward to see her enjoying herself in that way.

I finally worked out a routine that I thought would be successful, even allowing for Lucy doing her own version, or perhaps not at all, as the case might be at the time.

It was time to put my mind to another challenge, introducing Lucy to the car. All my dogs travel well and it was therefore important that Lucy should be able to join us all on our outings.

I started by opening all the doors of the car, I took a book and sat on the back seat reading. I took no notice of Lucy at all. I had kept all the other dogs indoors, so that there would be no distractions. Lucy paced around and kept coming and looking in at me. I ignored her. The first time I did that I stayed for about 20 minutes. She did nothing more than pace around and occasionally look up at me. I did not acknowledge her at all. When I got out of the car I still did not look at her and walked back to the cottage. I repeated the same move for the next four days and made no attempt to do anything other than that, because if she happened to be looking in when I even turned a page of my book, she would go. I always left all the car doors open.

On the fifth day I had no book. I took some of her favourite chicken treats with me and again sat in the back of the car, with all the doors open. I said nothing to her. When she approached to look in, I put my hand down and held out a treat, which she eagerly took. I repeated that several times over the next three days, and I then moved into the middle of the back seat. Lucy came to see what was happening so I held out a treat, but kept it far enough away from her so that she had to put her front feet on the edge of the seat to reach it. She was not prepared to take part in this exercise.

I guessed that I was in for the long haul, so the following day I sat in the same position and took a newspaper to read. I then had to wait a further four days before she suddenly leapt on to the back seat, took the treat and leapt out again. After a further two days she was doing that without hesitating. I then kept one door shut and sat next to it, so that left the opposite door and the two front doors open. I had a treat in my hand and she jumped in, but the second that she realised she would have to move further onto the seat, she leapt out again, not only that but she would no longer even come near the door.

I left it for that day but the following afternoon I tried again. She reacted by taking a swift glance into the car and then wandered off somewhere. She did not come back, so I knew then that I would have to go back a step and sit in the middle to allow her an easy escape route. I did this for a further four days, and then she took me by surprise again and jumped in. She didn't come straight for the treat but sniffed at the back of the front seats, sniffed over the back seat and then took the treat. I quickly made another treat available to her, and she seemed quite happy just to sit there. Whilst she was taking the treat, I shuffled around and moved my legs, but she did not seem to be worried by that. After about five minutes she jumped out, but I felt really pleased by the progress we had made.

During the following few days she was then sitting next to me on the back seat quite happily. I distracted her with yet another treat, then shut the door. I thought that she might panic but she remained calm and the next morning I had her with me, I climbed through into the front seat. She got very agitated but I ignored her, sat for a few minutes in the driver's seat, then opened the door, leaving it open. I also opened the back door at the same time. She got out of the car immediately, but after that she would get into the back seat with the lure of her treat. I was then able to shut the door before getting into the front. She didn't panic, and I tried starting the engine. She paced up and down the back seat but I ignored her. I then moved the car forward a few feet before letting her out.

I was then gradually able take her for a short ride. I wouldn't say that she was relaxed, but she stayed in the one place and did not seem bothered by cars behind us. I was really pleased because Lucy hated to be confined and I had anticipated really big problems transporting her anywhere and certainly never thought that she would travel voluntarily.

I had been working with Lucy and Jimmy practicing various moves, and they were working very well together. Lucy got very excited when we trained and had started to perform her own moves within the routine without any prompting. She particularly liked to circle around us going backwards, which meant that she bounced around like a spring driven thing. She would still not let me touch her collar, and if I did she would scream. She did not mind being stroked on her chest, but would not tolerate any other part of her body being touched at all.

At the end of August, Darren and Suzie came at the weekend, with the intention of Darren videoing the routine I was hoping to do at the show with Jimmy and Lucy. We set everything up outside in the training field, whilst at the same time keeping Lucy's attention by giving her treats. Our friend Patti was staying with us at the time. Lucy had accepted her presence very well and during her stay had allowed Patti to stroke her, albeit briefly!

So we had a small audience for our trial performance. She was very wary of the presence of strangers, but after a few false starts we went through the routine and I must admit that I was delighted. It was so rewarding to see that she could keep focused for that length of time, without the lure of food. However, as soon as the routine was finished Lucy disappeared and could not be persuaded to go near anyone and in fact growled at Suzie's little boy, Rory. She did quieten down once Suzie picked Rory up, but obviously had not realised until then that humans could be so small.

During the remainder of the month we had several trips away from home, to introduce Lucy to new sights and sounds. It was difficult for us to imagine what that must have been like for her.

# 7

September was now upon us, the prospect of the show was getting closer by the day, and we were in a state of absolute chaos. Folks were dropping off bric-a-brac and books, which we hoped to be able to display outside on the day, weather permitting. On the subject of the weather, we were in an unsettled period, with some very wet and windy days.

With that in mind we had to accept that it was going to be necessary to put all the various stalls in the training shed, together with all the tables for refreshments, drinks and home-made cakes, etc. Several people had donated large assortments of books, so altogether that was going to take up a lot of room. We also had to consider all the entrants and their dogs for the various events. Wrestling with that problem, together with many others, caused me more restless nights.

A few days before the show was due to take place, there was a slight break in the weather, which enabled me to cut the grass in the training field. Once that was done I partitioned off the top end, which would be used by the entrants and their dogs, so that Lucy would not be too distracted by the scent and presence of other dogs. It would also provide us with an area in which we could work together at the lower end of the field. Not really knowing at that stage what might happen, I could only hope that my idea would work.

On the day before the show was due to take place, our son, Derek Junior was coming over from England, with a view to helping out with all the countless jobs that would need to be done, if the day was to be a success.

Prior to his arrival, we had purchased a small gazebo which would enable us to accommodate some of the people in for shelter, if needed. As with all these types of purchases, the advertisement on the packaging clearly stated 'EASY TO ASSEMBLE'. It was also noted that it had been made in China. We might have known that this in itself was a warning to the uninitiated. Derek and I laid out all the various parts, which consisted of an assortment of poles of varying lengths, joiners, clips, bits of canopy and the top cover. We also noted that there were pegs provided for keeping the assembled item fixed to the ground. This seemed like a good idea to us, as we can be subject to some fairly windy gusts from the North West on occasions.

The last thing that would be needed on the day of the show was for the locals to report a low flying gazebo passing over the local hostelry. It is worth mentioning at this stage, that on a good day the wind may just tease off a few dead branches and would pile up the leaves, but on a bad day it has been known to remove the odd shed roof, shift plastic chairs and tables to other parts of the garden and sometimes even over the fence into the bog.

On examining the aforementioned pegs, we noted that they were about five inches long. To put this into perspective, the training shed is some 24 feet long and has been anchored down in two places with straining wire, firmly fixed to 6 foot fence posts. We gathered from those diminutive dimensions, that the prevailing winds in downtown Beijing were obviously nowhere near as fierce as those that we were used to here in Ireland.

Having carried out a thorough examination of all the parts, checking quantities, etc. We then read the instructions. These would appear to have been rather loosely translated from Mandarin to broken English, as in one part of the instructions it referred to the fact that the gazebo, once completed, would be good for breaking wind. At that point we decided that enough was enough and we decided to leave the assembly for Derek Junior to tackle the following day. We had already told him about the gazebo, and he had told us not to worry, just leave everything to him. With that in mind we put all the bits back in the box and put it away. We should mention at that point our son has never been gifted with a great deal of patience, therefore lack of success on any particular project, however small, will usually bring on what one might describe as a mood, accompanied by the ability to further improve any bystanders grasp of the Anglo Saxon language, should they be within earshot.

The next morning dawned and it was an overcast day, with the rain falling gently, but persistently. Derek arrived home and once he had unpacked his bits and pieces and had some tea and toast, he said that he was ready to tackle anything that needed his attention. Derek and I smiled at each other and led Junior to the package containing the gazebo. At that stage it looked innocuous enough, but the challenge would come later. We said that we would leave him with it for a while, so he could familiarise himself with all the working bits, and we would watch progress from a distance, so that we did not get in the way. It should be noted that some of the poles were numbered from 1 to 8, some marked with letters from A to G, and the joiners, of different sizes, were not marked at all. Watching Derek Junior we could see that he was having difficulty with the English/Chinese instructions. He proceeded to cast aspersions on the translator and said that whoever was responsible for said translation left him, Derek Junior, questioning whether or not said Chinese person knew his parents.

To be fair to Junior, he had three attempts at getting the gazebo to resemble the picture on the box, but to no avail. At each attempt he became more cross, his language became more colourful and Derek and I collapsed with laughter. That only caused Junior to become more annoyed, and it was obvious that his patience was starting to evaporate. So, the three of us combined our efforts and together with the help of some strong duct tape, finally got the gazebo assembled and into position. We made up four suitable anchors, drove them firmly deep into the ground and pronounced the job well and truly done.

There were still many other little items to attend to and it was getting dark before we finished, having gone as far as we could. Anything else would have to be tackled on the following morning. Whilst Junior and I tidied up the odds and ends, Derek had gone into the cottage to start preparing a mountain of sandwiches and organise cold drinks. I had grave doubts in the back of my mind that even at this late stage the show might have to be cancelled, as it was still raining with no apparent signs of a let up. Another restless night was in store, as all I could hear on the bedroom windows was the sound of the rain, accompanied by a fairly strong wind. I questioned as to why I had picked this particular date? Why did it have to rain and blow on this, of all days? Why could we not get some sun here like they do in Spain?

By the time it got to about 5.30 am, I decided that I had had enough of wriggling and fidgeting about, so I decided to take the dogs for their morning walk and then be ready to face the day before the first show entrants arrived. I donned my wet weather gear and off we went. I knew full well that once the Show started, the dogs would have a long wait before they could have their freedom around the cottage again, so the early morning chase across the bog would do them good. The wind and rain might also help to clear my head, although I did have my doubts.

To further increase my fears, I received my first phone call on my mobile at 7.30am from folks down in Galway to tell me that it was raining cats and dogs there, (did I say that?) and asked would the show still be going ahead.

"Come on now," I said, trying to sound more confident than I really was,

"What's a drop of rain to people like us?".

I endeavoured to keep the first signs of hysteria out of my voice, but that was proving difficult. I was still walking back to the cottage and I was absolutely soaked to the skin.

When I got back to the cottage I found that Derek had also received several calls from folks who were worried about whether the show was on or not and had confidently told them all that, unless a typhoon or blizzard struck, the show would go ahead as planned. He was certainly not prepared to consign his mountain of refreshments to the ducks at this stage. You might get cold, wet and wind blown, but you would at least be full up.

The decision was made. We would carry on. So, come what may, there was still plenty left to do and certainly no time to dwell on the weather. The gazebo was still firmly fixed in place, so we started by turning all the plastic chairs upside down, in an attempt at least to keep the seats dry.

Our first morning helpers arrived at about 9am. We all gathered in the kitchen, drinking tea and watching the rain pelting down, without so much as a break. We had advised everybody that we would be starting at 10.30am, to give us time to get through a very busy programme of events and to leave enough time for a tea break and a chance for folks to bargain hunt amongst the bric-a-brac or further damage their waistline buying and then testing the variety of homemade cakes. At about 9.30 we made our way across to the training shed. That then provided another very good excuse to drink more tea and commiserate with one another about the abysmal weather conditions. By then we had received a stream of calls to ask if the

Show was still going ahead. We replied with great confidence that we would be doing so and that anyone who wanted to take the chance and join in was more than welcome. We also asked them to consider the fact that Ireland seemed to be one of those places that can experience all four seasons in one day, so there was at least a 25 per cent of them being able to top up their tan.

We were still standing in the shed, finishing off our tea, when from outside someone shouted,

"Everybody, come and see this!".

Once outside we could see what all the fuss was about. The rain had stopped, there was a clear blue sky, as far as the eye could see and the sun had put in a very welcome appearance. Within a space of just 30 minutes, the weather had changed from near monsoon conditions, to then match anything we ever experienced on our best summer days. We could not believe our good luck, and consequently everyone's spirits noticeably lifted.

The time was now nearing 10.30am, and we were preparing for the first class. I had noticed that before we left the cottage, Lucy appeared to be quite settled, despite the fact that we had had lots of strangers in the kitchen, the sound of cars arriving, and other dogs barking from time to time. Jimmy was more unsettled than Lucy was, and I then began to wonder what frame of mind both of them would be in, once faced with the prospect of entering the training field, to be met by some 70 strangers and their dogs, and then showing everybody what they could do, or not, as the case may be. I had learnt by that time that Lucy did not always react at the time to any changes, but would then sometimes become disturbed a couple of days after the event. Believe me, at this stage I was not fooling myself. I realised that I had given her a huge task to undertake, and cope with. Once I realised just how many people had arrived with their dogs and tried to imagine how Lucy would perceive this new experience, I admit to questioning my wisdom in exposing her to this. Could I have been accused of having assumed too much at this stage?

When we originally discussed holding a show of some sort, a Fun Dog Show was obviously an event that would or should appeal to a lot of dog minded people, but at the same time we did wonder what reception we would get, once invitations were officially sent out. We need not have worried. Practically everyone who was invited turned up and all more than ready to join into the spirit of things. It's funny, isn't it… put two strangers in a situation where they have to walk past each other, and you may get an acknowledgement and a one word greeting… put two people, who have never seen one another before, with their dogs and you need a crowbar to separate them... dogs... wonderful ice breakers!

Looking over the various events it was immediately obvious that each event had been well subscribed to, with plenty of entrants for each class. We started the show off with a competition for the Most Handsome Dog/Bitch, followed by classes including Best Trick and a Fancy Dress Competition, for the dogs, not the owners. We also played Musical Chairs, which meant that the dog had to sit on command before the owner could claim a seat. This led to great hilarity, not to mention the odd dog sitting on command, and the owner slipping off the side of the chair, then someone else taking over.

Derek was keeping a schedule of the winners, so that when the time came for the prize presentations everything would be organised. It was important that this went without a hitch, as the prizes were being presented by John Perry TD, (In Ireland a TD is the equivalent to an English Member of Parliament). He had volunteered to do this, as the money raised was to be given to a local charity, but had to interrupt a very tight schedule to fit us in and his time was therefore limited.

After the seventh event we stopped for refreshments and the break gave everyone a chance to have their sandwiches, try the lovely home made cakes, have a cup of tea or coffee and just enjoy the sunshine. For those that wished there was time to browse among the heaps of books, trinkets, pictures, CDs, and DVDs.

Suzie and I took this opportunity to go over to the cottage to collect Lucy and Jimmy. Lucy now appeared to be agitated and growled at Suzie, refusing to take a treat. Jimmy was very excited, so all in all things did not look too good at that stage. We sat quietly in the lounge, with a cup of tea and a sandwich, ignoring both of the dogs, waiting for them to calm down. After a few minutes they looked more relaxed, but then my nerves took over! Having spent time to allow Lucy and Jimmy to calm down, I then needed Suzie's help to enable me to do the same. A few minutes later, we took the two dogs over to join the others.

Prior to this I had already asked Derek Junior to keep everyone behind the ropes and seated at the far end of the training field. This was necessary, as I had no idea as to how either of the two dogs would react. Jimmy had never performed in front of a crowd, and Lucy of course was a completely unknown quantity.

I had previously taken the decision that it would be unwise to try to complete a full routine of Heelwork to Music, in the strict sense of the word and had decided just to play some restful music and let the two of them do a few moves of their own, then hopefully start working together, once they had settled.

As we entered the training field neither of them seemed to be unduly perturbed by the crowd, but they were both still on their leads at this stage. Derek and I had already arranged that when he saw me nod my head, he would start the music. I asked Suzie to keep Lucy on her lead, to one side of the field and at this point looked in Derek's direction and gave him the nod, having at this stage let Jimmy off his lead. The silence was deafening… no music… the crowd silent in anticipation…

I looked in Derek's direction again, put my thumb up and nodded; he looked at me and nodded, put his thumbs up… still nothing.

Whilst all this was going on, or not going on as was the case, Jimmy had sauntered off to do his own thing somewhere. Needless to say this did nothing to calm my already shredded nerves. I glanced over at Suzie and Lucy, and they both seemed to be quite cool, calm and collected. No reason for them not to have been, they weren't where I was. I had exhausted all my options and wondered just what on earth to do next when suddenly…MUSIC!

I called out to Jimmy, and he came straight to me with his usual enthusiasm, that is until he caught sight of Darren approaching the field boundary, with his camera and video equipment. This was something entirely new for Jimmy and called for immediate action. He bounded across to Darren, barking and growling as he went. I shouted out to Darren to tell him to let Jimmy see and sniff the camera, and once he was allowed to do this he was fine. He then returned to me, and at last we were able to make a start, having tendered my apologies to the waiting crowd for the delay.

Being doggie folk they all understood the problem that insofar as Murphy's Law was concerned, if it can happen then it will.

I proceeded to do a few simple moves with Jimmy, who was quite distracted by all the different noises, people and of course, their dogs. I then asked Suzie to let Lucy off the lead and I clearly remember thinking… here we go. Wonder of all wonders, she joined Jimmy and me and gave me her complete concentration. Surprisingly enough, she seemed to be more focused than Jimmy was and actually worked very well, considering the circum-stances. Prior to this Lucy had always shut down when other people and especially other dogs were around and then only did anything in very slow motion. I was so pleased with them both, but especially delighted with Lucy in that she had trusted me enough to work with me, in the close proximity of strange dogs and people, whereas before she would have been petrified.

The demonstration went very well, and the crowd applauded the efforts of the two dogs for a display well done. I thanked the crowd and then went back to the cottage, taking my two star performers with me for a 'jackpot' of chicken treats.

The demonstration over, it was then time to make a start on the remaining classes. It had been such a beautiful sunny day that it had encouraged most of the folks to seek drinks and snacks and enjoy just basking in the sunshine. Unfortunately, this did nothing to help the sales of the mountain of books, DVDs, and bric-a-brac that were spread liberally over many tables in the training shed. I knew that had it rained, they would have been driven by circumstance to browse between showers, but then that would have detracted from the success of the whole event. During the break John Perry arrived to award the prizes. All the dogs entered for the various events had originally been trained at my facility here, and I was especially pleased with their behaviour, considering that most of them had never been in a situation like that before. In the days following the show I received many phone calls and text messages, from both entrants and their friends, to say how impressed they were at how well behaved all the dogs had been. It was a great reward for me that people could have fun with their pets, without causing any problems, considering that the final total attendance was over 80 people.

After the prizes were presented, people then began to say their farewells and the friends that had stayed behind to help out on the day, sat for a well earned rest and …yes…another cup of tea. Now the dust had settled, I realised just how exhausted I really felt, but at the same time happy that the day had turned out so well for everyone and that everything had more or less gone without a hitch.

Once everyone had taken their leave, Derek Senior, Derek Junior and I returned to the cottage to give the dogs their tea. I was glad to see that Lucy appeared to be quite settled, after her 15 minutes of fame. It looked quite likely that yet another hurdle had been overcome that day.

The three of us had a bite to eat and then Derek Jnr and I went back to the training shed to make a start on dismantling tables, stack chairs and have a general tidy up.

Outside we tackled the dismantling of the gazebo, which didn't present the amusement that erecting it had done. Just as well really, as it is quite likely that Junior would have taken the next flight back to England.

The training field looked none the worse for wear, considering the amount of use that it had had that day. The final job was to wash over the training shed floor and leave everything shipshape ready for the next week's lessons. I switched off the lights, closed the doors and stood for a few brief moments in complete silence, reflecting on what could only be described as a truly great day.

# 8

Well now...not the case the following day. Lucy, true to form, was unsettled again. She urinated indoors, she ignored me completely and just paced up and down, in and out. She was disobedient and would not approach me. From past experience, I had learned that she never reacted at the time of any incident, it was always over the course of the following days that her change of behaviour manifested itself. I knew by then that I should have been prepared for her reactions, but nevertheless, it still perplexed me and caught me unawares.

Over the years that I have worked with dogs of varied breeds and backgrounds, I have never come across any dog that has displayed such delayed behaviour. Dogs live for the moment and whilst something or someone may trigger an unpleasant memory, causing a dog to react, the behaviour displayed by Lucy was so totally different.

Derek Junior was due to fly back to England that afternoon, so we took a little time out, had a very leisurely breakfast and had time to exchange various bits of news.

Meanwhile, Lucy continued her pacing back and forth, but we ignored her and left her to her own devices. When the time came for Derek to leave for the airport, he called Lucy to try to say goodbye, but she was having none of that. In the past she has occasionally flirted with young Derek, but on this occasion she was obviously not in an amorous mood.

We arrived at Knock International Airport with enough time for a drink and a snack with Junior, before it was time for the farewells at the departure gate. I know that no one relishes the thought of goodbye; what's the old saying… 'parting is such sweet sorrow'…and neither of us was any different from the rest, when it came to saying farewells to either of our children. It was essential that I armed myself with a good supply of tissues, as I knew what would happen once he was out of sight. I snuffled my way out of the terminal to the car park and then sat for a few moments, composing myself before the drive back home.

We had not been gone very long and as we only live about 20 minutes away from Knock, the dogs had not had long to wait for our return. As I opened the front door, I was greeted by a puddle, the second one of that day from Lucy. The whole of the downstairs was tiled, so fortunately no lasting damage was done, nothing that a damp cloth and a little disinfectant couldn't put right. I was left wondering once again as to just how long it would take her to settle down again.

After our son's departure and this latest setback from Lucy, I did feel that I must do something to cheer myself up, and what better way of doing this than to go for a long walk with my dogs. We set out across the boglands, avoiding our usual pathways, and this delighted all the dogs, especially Lucy, as she does enjoy eating peat.

Unfortunately we always suffer after the event, as she usually needs to go outside in the middle of the night, the peat having a moving effect on her. A small price to pay, if it helped to calm her down again. Sunny went off, determined to find each and every ditch that had water in it and then test the depth and give himself a generally good soaking. Once that had been accomplished, it was wise to give him a wide berth, as the next job in hand was to deliver a severe shaking of the coat, so woe betide anyone within range. Jimmy also liked the bog in his own way, because this gave him the chance to locate any small piece of peat and toss it into the air, repeatedly. Whilst all that was going on, I was trying to maintain a footing on the slippery surfaces, looking for firm ground to avoid filling my wellies with icy cold water. Altogether we were out for over two hours and by the time we returned to the cottage, Lucy had settled down again and there were no further pacing incidents that day.

The following morning, I noticed immediately that she was still settled, but at the same time did not seem to want anyone near her. I decided that another long walk was going to be the order of the day. All went extremely well up to the point where

I rejoined one of our familiar tracks. Things felt a trifle uncomfortable under foot and I realised that one of my socks had gradually worked its way down under my wellie, something I am sure you have all experienced, on more than one occasion, if you are a dog walker. Anyway, I paused by the nearest tree, so that I could gain some support from it, whilst removing the wellie. Then… the unexpected happened.

As I bent down to pull up my sock, Lucy grabbed my arm, as she had done before, with her front legs and the strength that she exerted was really very powerful. She held me in a fixed stare and her expression, as had happened in the past, changed completely. My arm was hurting from the pressure that she was using, and I was feeling pain in my back, due to the rather unusual position that I then found myself in. Plus I had one wellie off and then a very wet foot. I called out to Sunny. He came over, looked at us both, walked around us a couple of times, decided that this had nothing to do with him and off he went. I then called out for Jimmy, but I could tell that he was not sure what he was supposed to do and decided that he would be better off just staying where he was.

This was now getting beyond a joke, so it was time to call out to Sunny again. I hoped that this time it might prove a distraction to Lucy and break her concentration… just the opposite! As Sunny approached she bared her lips to show her canine teeth. This was not something that I had ever witnessed her doing toward other dogs. Her pupils were dilated and her eyes looked really large. Sunny looked at me as if seeking some sort of guidance about what to do next, but I ignored him and turned away from him, hoping he would not react adversely to Lucy's behaviour, bearing in mind that at this stage she was still firmly attached to my arm. After a few more moments of weighing up the situation, he wandered off again, leaving me to contemplate my predicament, whilst viewing the greenery underfoot. I was also hoping that I would be able to straighten out my back, once the Mexican standoff was over. It was about that time that I had to remind myself that a dog is an animal… it is far too easy to treat them as if they were another human being, but I had witnessed just how quickly a dog could exhibit unexpected and unwanted behaviour, which could so often lead to tragic consequences.

Five minutes passed by and Lucy then decided that she would let go. She wandered off as if nothing had happened, leaving me to nurse my bruised leg and aching back, the latter showing the signs of the passage of time. It did take a little while for me to straighten up completely, and I knew that I would be suffering twinges for the next two or three days. I walked slowly back to the cottage, reflecting as I went about the chain of events that had led up to the latest incident and pondered yet again as to what her reasons might be for displaying that very unusual type of behaviour.

For the remainder of the day Lucy was fine and came to me immediately when I called her for her bit of fussing in the evening. I could sense that she was completely calm again.

I had been giving some thought to the fact that I would have to take Lucy over to the vets at Boyle in the not too distant future, as arrangements would have to be made for her to be spayed, so it was my intention to give her a trial run. The round trip would be about 45 – 50 miles, a good test of her travel abilities. I did not want her to suffer any adverse reaction to the trip, after having been spayed, so better to find out by doing a dummy run. By doing that I hoped, on the day, she would be in a more or less settled state, which was more than was going to be said about me.

During the following week a day presented itself where the diary had a few gaps and the weather was good, so off we went. When she first got into the car she appeared to be a little unsettled, but after a few minutes she calmed down and curled up on the back seat and stayed there until we arrived at the vets some half an hour later. I put her lead on and walked her from the car, across the car park and into the waiting room. I made the moves in a positive manner, did not hesitate and she did not protest. Suzie met us in the reception area and immediately offered Lucy a treat. Lucy took it without hesitation, albeit that she had to stretch her neck out like a giraffe. No one need think for one moment that they were going to get their hands on her by offering something as simple as a treat.

From the reception area, we then took her into the operating room and allowed her to have a sniff around. I then lifted her onto the operating table and she did seem to be a little unsure about that. She tucked her tail between her legs, but this did not stop her from taking further treats from either of us. Suzie then produced her clippers and showed them to Lucy and then held them against her front leg. There was no response. She then lifted Lucy's leg. Lucy averted her eyes, but allowed Suzie to do that, so Suzie tried once more without any problem. I lifted her down from the table and walked her back to the waiting room. A lady passed us by in the waiting area, but Lucy took no notice of her. I led her outside and gave her a chance to have a walk around. She took the opportunity to empty her bladder and appeared not to have been too bothered by the afternoon's happenings. She was a little reticent about getting back into the car again, but once on the back seat settled down, curled up and went to sleep.

The journey home was uneventful, so we decided that as she was settled, we would go into our local Supervalu store, get a paper and a few bits and pieces in the food line. I stayed in the car with Lucy, as the car park was very busy, with cars coming in and going out, people passing by our car with their shopping trolleys and quite a few boisterous youngsters seeking cold drinks and ice cream, as school had just finished for the day. Lucy just sat up and watched the entire goings on, seemingly interested, but certainly not bothered in any way. When Derek returned, we left the car park and made our way back home. Lucy was still settled and fine once we went indoors, and she ate her tea quite happily. Later that evening she did start to pace up and down again and continued doing this for about an hour. She then took up her usual place at the top of the stairs, on the landing.

At about 10pm I was at the top of the stairs and she approached me and I immediately sensed that there was something wrong. Fortunately our stairs turn through a 180 degree sweep to the left, and I was able to put the banisters between Lucy and me. I just knew that had I not done so, it was her intention to grab my leg again, given the opportunity.

The following day she was fine again and I spent ten minutes with her in the training shed. I had reached the stage where I was trying to teach her to walk with me without the lead and also to lift her left leg on the command 'left'. She really seemed to enjoy the little session, and it actually took some persuasion to get her to go back to the cottage.

I then took Sunny and Jimmy over to the training shed, but when I returned to the cottage some 20 minutes later, Derek informed me that a few moments after I left, Lucy had started to howl and had kept this up for over a minute. He said that he had never heard anything like it before and that it wasn't the same howling she made when Molly was buried. He did say that it felt quite eerie and that he had been worried as to what she might do in my absence. I could tell that he had been rather unnerved by the experience. The behaviour also had a similar effect on our little dachshunds, Billie and Carrie, as they both hid themselves under their blanket in their bed. Up to this day I have never been able to offer up an explanation for that particular behaviour. Over the course of the next few days, Lucy progressed really well with her training Her heelwork off the lead was excellent and she would sit on command instantly. She would also offer her left paw, again on command, back around me in a circle and also go through my legs, whilst I was walking forwards.

At last the day arrived for Lucy to make the trip to the vets at Boyle to be spayed. It was time to find out if the practice run had been worthwhile and that it would at least help her in some way to cope with the journey, without becoming too agitated.

As it was the day had not started out too well for me. I had woken up at about 5am to the sound of strong winds and the fierce pounding of heavy rain upon the bedroom windows. Added to that was my overall concern for Lucy's well being, during and after her operation and how she would react afterwards, so being up and about seemed to be a much better option than just laying in bed, worrying and waiting for the time to pass.

The first job of the day, before preparing breakfast, was to let the dogs out, which I did. The wind was still gusting, and although the rain had eased off, it was not a very nice start to the day. Another problem then presented itself. Neither of us was aware that the strong winds during the night had taken one of our outside gates completely off its hinges. The gate in question led from our enclosed outside area at the rear of the cottage, directly into the compound which contains the ducks and hens. Not realising this, I opened the back door and called the dogs in. The sound of my voice is usually enough to get them competing for the title of who gets indoors first, so I was surprised when…. no dogs. It was not unusual for one of them to scent out the occasional mouse under one of the sheds, and of course once one sniffed then everyone had to have a sniff. That was then followed by a lot of frantic scratching and digging in a vain attempt at unearthing one of the tiny visitors, who by that time was long gone. However there was not a dog in sight. What I did see, which caused my heart to skip several beats, was the remains of the gate lying in pieces on the ground, affording access to the whole area that contained our feathered stock and which normally would have been out of bounds to our four legged friends. Knowing that Lucy was a scavenger, I did not dare to try and guess what she has been able to gain access to, in the way of chicken pellets and household scraps, etc. which were all very nice for the ducks and hens, but not designed to go hand in hand with pre-operative necessity of nil by mouth.

As her operation was scheduled for later that morning, all food had been banned since the previous evening, so what I did not want was Lucy with a tummy full of assorted items of food. Fearful of the worst, I called Lucy and she came indoors immediately, followed by Sunny and Jimmy. Once they were inside the kitchen, I then returned to the field to see if there was anything obvious that Lucy might have eaten. The rainy weather during the night had proved to be a blessing, as it had washed away all traces of pellets and bread scraps, and I was not able to see anything that she might have had access to. For my own peace of mind I did call Suzie later that morning, to tell her of the events, but she felt that there would have been no damage done that might have affected the anaesthetic.

So we set off for Boyle, allowing enough time in case of any unforeseen problems that might happen on the way, and when we were over half way, there it suddenly dawned on me that I had left my camera behind. Photographs were going to play a very important part in Lucy's life records, as they would provide a pictorial reference for all the major happenings along the way.

So, we made an emergency stop at the first filling station that we came to, and I was able to buy one of those cameras that you use once and throw away. Never having had experience of that type of camera, I was not too sure as to how good the photos would be, but it would have to do. At a time like that any camera was better than none. We set off once more and surprisingly enough arrived at Suzie's surgery with a little time to spare. I took Lucy inside immediately and Suzie injected her with a sedative. I could see that Lucy was not at all impressed, but once I lifted her onto the table she settled down and sat with Suzie, as good as gold, waiting to have her photograph taken. Any onlooker might well have been forgiven for assuming that the little dog was used to being in the limelight, instead of which she was a dog that had never been subjected to anything like that before, having been denied any contact with humans from an early age.

After the sedative had been administered, Suzie put her into a cage, and it was then time for Derek and I to leave. Suzie said that she would send me a text to let me know when everything was alright, so we headed for the nearest café for two cups of their strongest coffee. To be fair to Derek, he was his usual calm and collected self, whereas I was nearly airborne. We decided to pass a little more time, by going to one of the local supermarkets and getting a few essentials. Derek's way of dealing with situations like this is to do what he is good at… buying food.

Anyway, I sped around the supermarket, putting various items into the trolley, mostly items that we did not need or want and forgetting items that we could have done with. Whilst I had been doing that, Derek had contented himself at the magazine rack, but once he saw what was in the shopping trolley, he took over, went back around the store, returned all the items that we didn't need and loaded up the stuff that we did want. Aware that I had not been a great deal of help, I suggested another cup of coffee. My philosophy is… if in doubt… drink, whereas Derek's is… shop. Before you think how lucky to have a husband who likes retail therapy, his idea of shopping fun is for… that's right… food.

It was then getting close to midday and Suzie sent a text to say that Lucy's operation had been a success, that she was fine and back in a cage. I was so relieved to hear the news that I could not get back to the surgery fast enough. Once there we spent some time talking to Suzie and Sinead and looking at their new kennels and cattery, which was scheduled to be opened within the next few days. Suzie went back into the surgery to check on Lucy's progress and she was fully awake, lying quietly in her cage. She would not get up to walk, so Suzie carried her out to the car, placed her on the back seat on her blanket and she slept soundly all the way home.

She was still settled and quiet when we arrived back at the cottage and later that evening woke up and ate all her tea. She was reluctant to go outside, but I remained with her until she had finished her toilet and once back inside, she slept soundly for the rest of the evening.

At bedtime she appeared to be very restless, so I stayed awake in case she might suffer an adverse reaction. Based on the recent past, Lucy always had a delayed reaction to the events of the day, so I was concerned that it might well be the case again and that unusual or agitated behaviour might be displayed, when we were least expecting it.

All went well during the night and the next morning she seemed fine, although she was still a little reluctant about going outside. I noticed that she also wanted physical contact with me at every opportunity, something hitherto unknown. I remained with her when she went into the front garden, but she then spent a lot of her time just hiding under the trees and the bushes. Other than that the day passed without incident.

I left the cottage for my usual early morning walk with Sunny and Jimmy. Just as I was shutting the front door Lucy started to howl, and I could still hear her as we walked up the lane. I spoke to Derek after the walk and he said that he had tried everything to distract her, but she was having none of it and kept up her howling for the entire one and a half hours that I was out for the walk.

Whilst she was doing this, Derek had tried to maintain some level of sanity by putting on his headphones and listening to a few of his old rock classics. He did say that her howling didn't go down too well with the likes of Pink Floyd and Status Quo, but what more could he do?

Once I returned to the cottage she stopped and settled down again. After lunch I took her into the front garden on her own, and as soon as she was through the front door, she headed purposefully away down the front garden, through the bushes. I took my time in following her and when I finally reached her, I found her sitting under a bush alongside Molly's grave. Momentarily I thought that was strange, but put it down to coincidence. I called her to me, but she remained sitting, just staring at me. I called her again, but she made no attempt to move. I did not feel at all happy about leaving her there alone, at that stage, for any length of time, so I went indoors for her lead, put it on her and very gently tried to coax her away. She immediately started to howl again. It was not like the howl that she had made when Molly was being buried, but nonetheless, I did find it very disturbing.

I walked slowly back to the cottage, and she continued to howl until we reached the front door. As soon as I opened the door she stopped. Once inside the cottage she seemed to be perfectly alright and made for her favourite resting place, curled up and went to sleep. I was left to wonder whether it was a coincidence that she had howled because she had reached the place where Molly was buried, or was it because she objected to me moving her. I did wonder whether there might be a deeper meaning to all this. Would she repeat this behaviour the next time she was let out, or would it be just a one off occurrence? It had to be said that if nothing else, Lucy certainly kept me on my toes and always gave me plenty to think about.

Later that day I let her out with Sunny and Jimmy. I watched carefully to see if she was going to head for Molly's place, but once she had relieved herself she stayed close to me. From that time on, I have never seen her return to the site of Molly's grave.

That same evening, after tea, I let Sunny, Jimmy and Lucy into the front garden. It was very quiet and still quite warm, and it was my intention to go out with them. As I was about to do so, the telephone rang, so I decided to take the call and follow the dogs into the garden, once I had dealt with the caller. The entire conversation only took about five minutes, but when I got outside Lucy was nowhere to be seen. Sunny and Jimmy were rooting about among the trees and bushes, as usual, but... no Lucy.

There was a good half an acre of front garden that had been given over to well established trees and shrubs, so I commenced to search frantically for her. There was no way that she could have got outside of the cottage confines, as the fencing surrounding the cottage is mostly over four feet high and not something that Lucy could jump over.

I eventually located her under one of the larger bushes and found that she had actually dug a den just large enough to conceal herself. I got down on my hands and knees so that I could be at her level and show her that I posed no threat and called her to me. It was immediately obvious that she had no intention of leaving her den. One of the main reasons that I wanted to keep a close watch on her was because I did not want her chewing away at her stitches. Up to that point she had shown no interest in them. To give credit where it was due, Suzie had done a really marvellous job with the suturing, and I had to look very closely to see the wound. Not invisible, but as near as you were ever going to get.

I felt at that stage it might be better to leave Lucy in her little den, as she was obviously finding comfort in it, but I was also aware that I would have to fetch her in before dusk, in case she decided to hide elsewhere. When I later went back to her, it did appear that she had not moved. I reached down and slowly eased her out of her den, clipping her lead on at the same time.

She offered no resistance and came with me quite quietly back to cottage, almost as if we had just returned from a long walk.

Once through the door she made straight for her usual place at the top of the stairs, and within a few moments was fast asleep. At that point I was left wondering what the next day would bring.

# 9

In the morning Derek and I were due to go to Sligo, so I let Lucy out of the back door of the cottage, as I did not want her disappearing into her new den, or anywhere else for that matter. She appeared not to be too bothered, and after taking the morning air, she came back inside and settled down with Sunny and Jimmy, as usual.

We got back from our shopping trip just before lunch and as soon as I opened the front door all three of them raced past me, into the front garden. I went into the lounge to check the phone to see if there were any messages and noticed that there were bloodstains where Lucy had been lying, also more stains on the tiles. I immediately called the dogs back indoors. Lucy jumped up onto her cover on the settee. She offered no resistance when I went to examine her.

To my dismay, I noticed that she had managed to pull a loop of flesh through the stitches, despite the fact that they still looked intact to me. There was no more that I could do, so it was time to call Suzie and tell her what had happened. She told me to take her straight over to the surgery and she would meet us there.

Derek drove, I stayed in the back of the car with Lucy. She now appeared to be very agitated, and it took me all my time to keep her away from gnawing at the wound area. As soon as we arrived at the surgery Suzie examined her and said that she was very relieved to note that the loop of flesh was not part of her intestine. It would appear that Lucy had managed to remove the internal sutures, and there was two inches of momentum protruding. Suzie administered an anaesthetic, removed the damaged tissue and then re-sutured three layers of the wound. Finally she put a body bandage around her, which would have been almost impossible for her to remove.

Yet another experience that unsettled Lucy, because when we returned to the cottage, all she would do was to pace up and down, crying and howling. That continued almost nonstop for the next four hours. Eventually, she calmed down and by the time we went to bed she was fast asleep. I was not aware of her moving at all during the night.

The next morning I took her for a gentle walk, but kept her on a long line. My instincts told me that she would take the first opportunity to disappear into the forestry to hide. If she did that, then my chances of finding her would be very slim. Recalling her recent behavior, together with the howling and den making episode, taught me that I must never underestimate the great influence that genetic makeup can have on a dog's behavior.

The following two days passed without further incident. She enjoyed her daily walks, and thankfully, had taken no more notice of the body bandage. On the eighth day following her operation, I considered that it was about time to let her off her lead once more. That was achieved without any problem, although she did run a long way ahead, something she had never done before. She had always preferred to stay just behind me. She did seem to be a lot more contented in herself, and much more settled.

On the ninth day I took Lucy back to the surgery in Boyle, for Suzie to remove the bandage and check the wound. Her skin was very sore where the bandage had been making contact, so Suzie suggested that it might be better to leave the bandage off altogether. Both Suzie and I felt that by that time Lucy would have lost interest in the wound and would no longer try to disturb it. However, nobody had told Lucy.

Immediately we returned to the cottage and got back indoors, she started grabbing at the stitches again. Once again I had to dress the area. I then had to keep her under constant supervision and change the dressing on a regular basis. Her skin was looking very red and sore and small blisters were starting to appear.

At that point in time I decided to change the type of dressing. The area along the stitches was very inflamed and she was still persisting in her attempts at removing them. Between us we managed to thwart her attempts at further sabotage. After another four days the skin surrounding the wound looked much less angry, and she appeared to have lost interest in the stitches. Four days after that we were able to have the stitches removed. Everything was going along exceeding well, and I did feel another obstacle had been overcome, yet another traumatic episode in Lucy's life was drawing to a close.

Wrong again. The very next morning Lucy chewed along the line where the stitches had been and made it bleed. It did not look as if she had caused any major damage and she appeared to be full of fun, so I took her, Sunny and Jimmy for a long walk. She raced around and actually invited Jimmy to play. I had never witnessed this type of behavior before from Lucy, and I think that Jimmy might just have been happy to oblige her, had it not been for Sunny coming up to him, causing him to back off.

The following week, Jean, an old friend of ours from England, came over to stay with us for a holiday. She managed to do this every year. It was nice to see her and talk about all the changes that had taken place in our old home county of Hampshire, since we left in 1998. Jean is a very enthusiastic walker, so we were able to go on many walks with the three dogs and Lucy loved that. During those times she was still trying to encourage Jimmy to play, but each time Sunny put a stop to it. What a spoil sport.

At about that time she added to her repertoire of funny behavior. She would race around and suddenly come up to us and perform one of her heelwork to music moves, such as backing around me in a circle. We gave her no encouragement whatsoever, but it was such a joy to watch her and laugh at her totally unrehearsed performance. She was still occasionally chewing at the site of the old wound, but she was very easily distracted and caused no further damage. I never bothered trying to do any form of training with the dogs whilst we had visitors.

When Jean was with us it gave us time to visit different places and also an excuse to try out some of the exceedingly good restaurants in the Sligo region. All good things had to come to an end, and the week seemed to fly by. It was time for Jean to return to the UK, time for us to get back into our routine again and for me to resume training.

We had now arrived at the stage where Lucy would walk anywhere without her lead and was keeping to heel. She sat, without a command, when I stopped and would come to me instantly when I called her. She would also drop down next to me on command. Naturally, being the complete lady, she would not go down if the grass was wet, but was quite content to sit. I had been teaching her to stay, providing I was not too far away. This was an exercise that had to be taught in very slow stages. It had to said that she was quite happy to obey all these various commands, providing there were no other distractions. If there were, then I could be totally ignored and she would not even tolerate being stroked. She still did not like the lead being put on her and refused to come near me if she saw it. She screamed sometimes when I took hold of her collar. It was for that reason I did not want the use of a plastic collar after she was spayed, as I considered that it might be too much of an unpleasant experience for her.

At long last Lucy appeared to have lost all interest in the site of her wound, so, another problem behind us. I did notice that she was getting more adventurous on our daily walks and was venturing short distances into the forestry to explore. On the one hand I had become so very used to her being close to me all the time, but on the other it was such a pleasure and so rewarding to see her extending her boundaries. It meant that she had accepted that I would always be nearby if she needed me. Lucy had by that time developed a passion for blackberries. On one of our walks there is an abundance of bushes, usually heavy with fruit, through all the summer months. Although she consumed far more that I ever could, it did not seem to cause her any problems with her digestive system.

The next visitors to arrive were our friends Bernard and Chris, who came from Dorset. They were staying for three weeks and always brought several miniature Dachshunds and a couple of Borzois. There's a combination if ever there was one. They all stayed in the larger of our two mobile homes, which is fully equipped with all mod cons. That enabled them to come and go as they pleased during the day and also served to keep their dogs separated from ours.

They arrived mid afternoon. Once they had unpacked and settled their dogs, they came over to the cottage for a cup of tea, to discuss their trip from the UK to us. Their usual route was to take the ferry from Fishguard to Rosslare and then take their time by coming at a leisurely pace by way of the west coast. We noticed that Lucy was very wary of them when they came in, she would not venture near them. However, she did not growl.

That same evening when we went to bed, she appeared to be a little more unsettled than usual, and we attributed that to the fact that there were strange dogs present on what she perceived as her territory.

The following morning Chris and Bernard were outside the mobile home with their dogs. The entire area is securely fenced, so there was absolutely no danger of any of their dogs getting out, or of any of ours getting in. As soon as I opened the front gate of the cottage, Sunny and Jimmy raced over to greet the newcomers with their usual exuberance, but Lucy was not at all impressed. She barked at Chris, Bernard and their dogs, growled and then up went her hackles. I stayed and had a chat with them for quite a while and very slowly Lucy edged her way towards us. As she came closer, Bernard reached over the fence, and Lucy thought that he had a treat for her, so he was able to touch her briefly, but as soon as she discovered that there was no treat to be had she quickly moved away again.

It took another five days before Lucy stopped reacting to the presence of their dogs. For the remainder of their stay she took no further notice of them whatsoever. She refused to make eye contact with either Chris or Bernard and would not approach them until their final day, just as they were ready to leave. Then she allowed them to stroke her, just before they went out the front door.

That simple move went to prove once again that Lucy would always dictate who she would approve of and who she might not. After they left she returned to her usual resting place, whilst Derek and I went outside to say our final farewells. It seemed very quiet once they had gone after having had their company, with all their dogs, for the last three weeks. However it did not take very long to settle once again into our daily routine and life returned to normal.

On the day before Chris and Bernard left, I had to remove a tick that had become embedded in my leg, just behind my knee. It did not take very long for the bite to become infected, and the leg started to swell. It became very painful, so it meant a quick trip down to see Dr Mike, for a course of antibiotics. Over the course of the next few days I was in a lot of pain, also it was agony just to try to walk. It left me feeling quite unwell generally. Needless to say neither Jimmy nor Sunny appeared to be aware of my discomfort but Lucy, on the other hand, was immediately conscious that something was wrong, sensing the change in me. She started to pace up and down, then she started to chew her feet. I could tell that she was anxious, as she would not sleep in her usual place and remained as restless as I was for the next three nights. Once I had finished the course of antibiotics, I soon returned to normal, and Lucy did the same.

September gave way to October, with thoughts of the impending time change, which would mean less daylight and longer nights. We were still getting a good amount of sunshine most days, with very little rain. Towards the end of the month, just before summertime ended, I was out on my usual walk across the bog, when I was confronted by a horse and rider. None of my dogs had ever encountered a horse before at close proximity. Sunny immediately started to bark, so I called him away, but surprisingly enough Jimmy and Lucy were very well behaved. I was very pleased with their reactions, as it was not often that we ever met anyone at all on our morning rounds. Part of our six acres extended along a good length of one of the lanes, and I am convinced that Sunny especially considered that the whole of this land was his territory. Heaven help anyone who should even dare to set foot on it. He was prepared to permit the occasional rabbit, fox, hare or even badger to cross the land, even a partridge now and again, but certainly nothing as big as a horse! October ended without further incident. November heralded once more the short days and long evenings.

Fortunately, where we live, in the north west of Ireland, we do get very long summer days, with day breaking at about 4am and continuing until well past 10 o'clock in the evening. The downside of course was that the mornings in winter remained very dark until quite late and darkness fell quite quickly again in the afternoon, until it all changed once again with the shortest day in December.

In the days following Bernard and Chris's departure, I did notice that Lucy was reacting badly towards any of our friends that called. She appeared to have gained a lot of confidence over the last few weeks and was beginning to assert herself at times. She would not settle and would growl continuously, if strangers were present, so I decided that, should someone call, I would put her on her lead and keep her behind me. That would give our callers a chance to go into the lounge and sit down. I was then able to take Lucy into the lounge, where she would settle down immediately, next to me, without any fuss. She would still growl if anyone moved, more so if they made eye contact with her. We had already cautioned all our friends about the need to ignore her, but that proved rather difficult at times, as we only have a small lounge. In the majority of cases it worked and that was the best that we could hope for. I was still very mindful of the fact that both Lucy and Molly had become very territorial about the small mobile home and I did not want a repeat performance of that type of behavior in the cottage. I made it the golden rule that Lucy should be offered a treat by any visitors, but only when she was quiet and settled.

For the remainder of November I concentrated on working with Lucy on her heelwork to music routine, because I could tell that she was getting a lot of pleasure from doing that. It opened up fresh opportunities to teach her new moves and it was so rewarding to see her so very eager to learn.

Sometimes we worked together, at other times I would work with Lucy and Jimmy. When Jimmy was there Lucy always appeared to hold back a little and carried out her movements more slowly. This appeared to be very deliberate, and I wondered if it was her way of letting me know, that if I wanted the best out of her for the routine, then I should be prepared to give her my undivided attention and not share her time with Jimmy.

November drew to a very uneventful close. It was then time to start thinking about Christmas, which, as usual, had a habit of suddenly creeping up on me and finding that I was completely unprepared for it. I received a short sharp salutary lesson when one of the radio announcers blithely stated that there were only some 22 shopping days left to go.

Derek Junior had made arrangements to drive over for the Christmas break. Derek and I were so looking forward to that. I had a picture in my mind of a blazing log fire in the lounge, the three of us together and the dogs all laid on the fireside rug, no one able to move after having eaten one of Derek's superb turkey dinners, served up with all the trimmings, to be followed by the traditional lighting of the brandy on the pudding. Then, sitting and enjoying a good glass of whisky and ginger ale. This surely is just what Christmas dreams are made of.

Needless to say that November and December evening walks were done with the aid of torchlight, which did not seem to bother the dogs at all. It was not a time of the year that I liked, with the days being so short. I am very fortunate in that I do have a large indoor training facility, which enables me to work with the dogs on a daily basis, if the weather is against us. However there is nothing to take the place of a good long walk across the countryside and bog land, where the dogs can have the freedom of the outdoors. The enjoyment of fresh scents, moist grass and soft peat beneath their feet and the ability to go where they please. There was no substitute for ditches full of water and for Sunny this gave him the added bonus of being able to wade about as much as he liked in them, up to his neck.

It was a great blessing that neither Jimmy nor Lucy ever showed any inclination to do that, in fact just the opposite. Neither of them liked water that much and would do all they could to avoid, even the smallest of puddles. Sunny, on the other hand, usually returned from his walks as black as the Ace of

Spades and bearing in mind that he has a long coat, took several minutes with the hosepipe, to make him at least clean enough to be allowed into the kitchen.

# 10

The first week in December was coming to a close, so I decided that it was time to put my thinking cap on and do something about Christmas cards and presents. The Christmas decorations had to be unearthed from the variety of unidentifiable boxes that they had been put into after last Christmas. I have always promised myself that when I take the decorations down next time, I will be totally organized. I will put all the baubles in one box, tinsel and the like in another, check that all the lights still work, as I put them all away in yet another box and the larger decorations on top of a wardrobe, in a safe place. A good idea, I hear you say. There is nothing like the fun that can be had by trying to find out which fairy light does not work, especially the type where you get one bulb go out and the rest fail to light! A challenge I am never prepared to undertake, it is a far simpler task to buy a complete new set for a few Euros, thus avoiding unnecessary stress.

The Christmas holiday would be especially busy this year, as the training calendar was still fairly full, and Derek Junior would also be arriving from England. I realised that Lucy had now been with us for eight months.

When I reflected on her progress and her rehabilitation during that time, I had to admit that in some directions my expectations had been exceeded, but there were other areas where little or no progress had been made at all. The whole business of living with Lucy had been a roller coaster of emotional ups and downs. She had this enigmatic attitude, whereby she could make me feel that what I was doing was all a waste of time, both hers and mine. She did not possess the power of speech, but was able to convey her feelings about most things, by just the way she looked at me. Because she made me feel that way, she also gave me the determination to think, research and experiment in other directions.

To gain the knowledge that I now possess about dogs, I have had to study over many years and have completed various courses in connection with the training and psychology of dogs, but there has been nothing to compare with the actual hands on experience. Nothing I had ever done, by way of practical learning, or from any books, could have prepared me for the challenge that Lucy and Molly had presented. I help people to train and rehabilitate dogs of all ages and breeds, every week, but now more than ever, I am beginning to question everything that I do. Lucy's presence has taught me to explore all avenues and to realise that if something does not work, that does not mean to say that it is necessarily a failure. It really offers me another opportunity to learn another approach to the problem.

It has never ceased to amaze me that even after all these years, I can and do, learn something new from each and every dog that I work with.

Like millions of others around the world, Christmas is a time for us to have friends visiting us, some who are regular local friends, others who live too far away that perhaps we only have contact with once or twice a year. I do confess that I really love the days leading up to Christmas, and this year was affording me the same degree of pleasure, added to the fact that we also had the arrival of Derek Junior to look forward to. We were now approaching the 16th December, which was a Saturday.

I was going to decorate the lounge, so I brought all the various boxes of bits and pieces downstairs. Lucy showed great interest and it didn't take me long to realise why. She would eat anything made of plastic, tin, metal or leather, and as I carried on unpacking the decorations she became more noticeably excited! She attempted, many times, to steal a bauble and any other trinkets that might be available. I had never seen her so eager to get something. It became a challenge to decorate the lounge, so that she couldn't reach anything. I was feeling quite pleased with myself by the end of the afternoon, with all the lights working, everything in place and the cottage now had that lovely Christmas atmosphere.

So, time for a cup of tea. I put the kettle on and called out to Derek, who had been upstairs attending to emails and the banking. When he came down stairs he said that, whilst he had been sat looking at the computer monitor, the sight in his left eye had become rather distorted. He said that it was like looking at a jigsaw puzzle, with the centre part missing. I suggested that perhaps he should contact the doctor for some advice, but as he was considering doing that, his sight returned to normal, and he thought that perhaps he had sat too long in front of the bright screen.

Whilst we were having our discussion and enjoying our cuppa, Lucy had taken the opportunity to rearrange the lounge decorations. We finished our tea and I asked Derek to come and see what I had done with the decorations. When we walked into the lounge we were met by the sight of Lucy trailing tinsel around, crunched up baubles and more tinsel chewed up and left in thousands of small pieces stuck in the rug. A Father Christmas had also been displaced and was minus his head. My primary concern was that Lucy might have eaten something that was sharp, but I could see that she had been more than content, going from one thing to another, on a seek and destroy mission. For the remainder of the festive season the lounge door was kept firmly shut.

The next evening we were entertaining. Derek was in great form, enjoying the company and it seemed to be a sign that a good Christmas was in store for us. The following morning, I rose as usual ready for another day, with not too much planned, apart from a couple of lessons, which would give me some time to attend to the writing of Christmas cards, wrapping presents in time for the post for those friends and relatives abroad and allow an hour or so for a walk with the dogs, as the weather was still being extremely kind to us. I sat quietly for a few moments, finishing my cup of tea. I decided to take one up to Derek, who was having a lay in, reading his book. I put the cup down on his bedside table and he said that he had a funny sensation in his left leg. For a couple of years he has experienced some pain and discomfort with his right hip, due to arthritis, so I immediately wondered if that might have something to do with it. I asked him if he meant his right leg and he replied,

"I may be getting old, but I can still distinguish my left leg from my right."

He said that his vision was again blurred in his left eye. I asked him exactly what he meant by that and he said it was the same fractured vision that he had experienced on the previous day. He was very unsteady on his feet, when he went to get out of bed, but he insisted on trying to get downstairs to the lounge. He managed to do that unaided, but it was very obvious to me that all was not as it should be.

I wasted no more time and immediately called our local GP, Dr Mike Fox, not sure whether or not I would be able to get him before morning surgery. As luck would have it he was on duty and once I described Derek's symptoms, he said that he would come up straight away. I was also trying to persuade Derek to sit still, as he was insisting that he should try to get up to see if he was able to control the movement of his left leg. He also told me that his left arm felt funny and would not go in the direction that he wanted it to. Thankfully Mike arrived a few minutes later. I sat on the settee, whilst he took Derek's blood pressure and carried out a few reflex tests. I was now approaching the point where I was going to cease to breathe, waiting for some indication from him as to what might be the matter. However, what did he say?

"You know that new car of mine, well, I have a problem with the rear parking sensor, as it seems to have developed a mind of its own. It is not functioning as it should do, and one doesn't expect that sort of fault to develop on a nearly new car."

At this point in time my blood pressure must have reached record levels and for one moment I was wondering if this was some new ploy of his in an attempt to rustle up more new patients. If so, he could be guaranteed that I would be somewhere very near the top of the list. He carried on to describe in greater detail the peculiarities of the wayward sensor in question and just to put the finishing touch to everything, it appeared that Derek was quite happy to join in the conversation. I was left wondering if in fact it was all part of a very bad dream and that I had, by mistake, joined in a car mechanics seminar. Somewhere around that time my colour started to turn from very pale to bright puce. Mike then produced his mobile phone, informing me, in a very matter of fact way, that he was fairly sure that Derek had experienced a "TIA (mini stroke) or…?"

Well, having been nursing in my earlier years, I knew very well what a TIA was, but what I didn't like was the bit at the end where he said "…or".

I could have done with a little more information with regard to Derek's diagnosis and a little less time discussing his blessed new car.

The telephone call that he made was to ask for an ambulance, and he told me that Derek would be taken into A & E at Sligo General Hospital, initially for assessment and then most likely would be admitted. At this stage, it was obvious that there was not a lot else that he could do, but as he picked up his bag he said,

"If anything happens before the ambulance gets here, then do not hesitate to call me immediately."

I replied, in a voice that was at least three octaves higher than usual,

"What do you mean, if anything happens… like what?"

I would have liked a lot more information, but none was forthcoming. I saw Mike to the door, told Derek not to even try to move and then proceeded to rush about the cottage like a headless chicken. Our cottage is only small, but I probably covered at least three miles in the next five minutes, trying to get my head around the latest course of events, at the same time gathering together all the necessary bits and pieces that I thought that Derek might need in hospital. For instance, I knew that we had an overnight case, but where was it? What about pajamas, dressing gown, his medication, something to read, his mobile phone and so on and so on.

Very soon the ambulance arrived and I learnt later that Mike had called them again when he got outside of the cottage. The ambulance that was on its way to us, asked if he had another ambulance there already. Mike replied,

"No, it is not another ambulance, it is my blasted faulty rear parking sensor that is giving trouble".

Anyway, the two paramedics came into the cottage and gave Derek a check over. They tested his grip, which they said was good, that he was fully aware of everything that was going on around him and that his speech had not been affected. I did not need them to tell me the bit about the speech, as I had already had proof that his speech was unaffected, after listening to the dissertation on cars delivered by Dr Mike and Derek's enthusiastic participation in the discussion about all things VW. Looking back I am glad to say that the discussions centered around new VWs. Can you imagine where the conversation might have led to, if Dr Mike had been a Microbus enthusiast? Imagine where the conversation might have gone if they had started to discuss the various merits of cookers, fridges and awnings! Sufficient to say that it would have been necessary for the ambulance men to find a place for me on board as well.

The paramedics took Derek to the ambulance, where they made him comfortable and hooked him up to various bits of technical equipment, so they could monitor him during the trip to the hospital, which is about 25 miles from our home.

One of them came to the cottage to tell me that they were off and that there was no need for me to rush, as Derek would have to be admitted to the hospital via A & E. I went back inside and tried to gather my confused thoughts into something resembling order, then prepare myself for what I could see was going to be a long day ahead.

The first job was to get the dogs settled, as they had never been used to being left for long periods of time, without one of us being around, and both Jimmy and Lucy were agitated. Jimmy had never liked the sound of any vehicle larger than the average family car. Once he heard the ambulance, that to him was definitely something bigger than a car. The sound of the diesel engine was enough to start Jimmy "singing". This involved starting off one octave above middle C and progressively moving up the scale to the point where ones ears start to ring, so two or three more decibels would no doubt be able to shatter wine glasses. There was also something about Jimmy's singing that dredged up some primeval instinct in all the other dogs, so we would end up with a combined noise output, which on a good day could compete with the massed bands of the Coldstream Guards.

The ambulance finally pulled away, I was able to quieten Jimmy down and then tried to act in an orderly controlled manner. That I was able to do until I telephoned my friend Sue. As I was speaking to her, it finally dawned on me just what had happened, my emotions took over and I broke down and cried. I was glad to be able to talk to Sue, as she proved to be a great help. She said that she felt that I was in no fit state to drive anywhere, let alone the 25 miles to the hospital, so she said that she would come over and take me in and stay with me, until such time as they were able to get Derek settled into a ward. She would never know just how very grateful I was for her help at that moment in time.

Before leaving for the hospital with Sue, I telephoned Derek Junior to tell him about his Dad, and he said that he would make plans to come over on the next available ferry. His ticket had already been booked, to cover the Christmas holiday, but once he explained the situation to the ferry company, they were more than happy to accommodate him on an earlier sailing.

Given all that had happened, we were still none the wiser as to what had actually caused the stroke, or how serious Derek's condition was. By the time that Sue and I arrived at the hospital, Derek had been taken away for X-Rays and other preliminary tests. It was mid-evening before he was finally admitted to a ward. We both went up to see him. He appeared to be quite settled, but I could tell that although he was making attempts at being cheerful, I knew that he was very concerned about what had happened.

We spent about an hour with him and it was then time to say our goodbyes. I promised that I would be in to see him as soon as I could the following day. Sue then took me back to the cottage, and after she left, I felt utterly drained and completely shattered by the unexpected events of the day.

In all the years that Derek and I had been together, we had never been apart for more than 48 hours. Things were just not the same without him being around. I carried on indoors and did all the jobs that were necessary, but they were all done by someone on autopilot, as my main thoughts were predominantly with Derek, wondering what the eventual outcome might be. I was not able to sit down for more than five minutes at a time, and I am sure that the dogs picked up on my restlessness as well. They knew that something was wrong and for a few hours at least Lucy had good company, as the other dogs all did their share of pacing up and down.

I finally looked at the clock and saw that it was 2am. I knew that I should try to get a few hours sleep but even after the exhaustion of the day took over, I found that sleep still did not come easily.

Both Lucy and Jimmy were very unsettled and Sunny was subdued. The next morning I got up at dawn and took them for their usual walk, but my thoughts were with Derek and what might lie ahead. I did not enjoy the walk at all, and I don't think that the dogs did either. Later that morning I made my way to the hospital.

I had not been there very long before Derek Junior arrived and his presence in itself made me feel a lot better, not feeling so alone to deal with the situation. We made our way to the ward, but by the time we got there, Derek had already been given a variety of different tests, including a CT scan and an ECG. I had to admit that my first impression was that he looked very well. His vision had returned to normal, but he was still very unsteady on his feet. He said that his left hand and left foot still felt funny. He said that he noticed that the grip in his left hand was almost non-existent and he described the sensation in his left foot as having a will of its own, not going where he wanted it to. When we finally had the opportunity to speak to the consultant, she said that she suspected that the stroke had been caused by a blockage in one of the carotid arteries.

For the next three days we continued to journey back and forth to the hospital. On the third day, Derek was given a

Doppler test on the arteries in his neck. The consultant arranged to meet us later in the day. She then confirmed that the stroke had been caused by a complete blockage of the right carotid artery. There also seemed to be some signs of a blockage of the left carotid artery. She followed that up with news that I found more disturbing. She felt that Derek may need an operation to clear the partially blocked artery. It appeared that this operation could only be performed at Galway University Hospital, which is over 70 miles away.

After giving us that news, she then said that Derek was alright to go home for Christmas. He would be provided with all the necessary medication that he would need to prevent anything untoward happening, until such time as he could be seen by the specialist consultant in Galway.

# 11

So, Derek came home, but within two days had developed a chest infection and was feeling unwell. He had lost what little appetite he had. Dr Mike prescribed a course of antibiotics, and Derek felt a lot better, despite the fact that the hospital medication was still upsetting him. We all muddled through Christmas as best we could, but it was an altogether very worrying time, however I had been glad of the support and companionship of Derek Junior.

I have mentioned before that Lucy is not a great one for change, and she had been subject to a lot of that over the last week or so, especially when Derek was in the hospital. Her regular routine had been disturbed, as I had been getting up earlier in the morning, so that all the dogs could have their usual run out, before I made my way to the hospital. It was not the same, as my heart was not really in it. I am sure that the dogs were all affected by my mood. Lucy, once again, was in a very agitated state and she then commenced trying to scavenge. That was something that she had not done for a very long time. In the past she had always been attracted by any tin, metal or hard plastic and had to be watched closely, as that type of detritus comes to the surface in the boglands. The moment that she was able to get hold of anything, then she would disappear. It was also proving difficult to get her to settle indoors, and she had reverted to more continuous pacing up and down. She also cried a lot as we left for the hospital, as prior to that she had never been particularly bothered by being left.

When Derek eventually returned home, despite the fact that we were now altogether again, she still appeared to be even more disturbed. Try as I might, I could not fathom out just what was going on, other than the fact that she shut down completely at times and then would not acknowledge anyone, not even me. She did return to her little den in the front garden and several times could be seen frantically scratching at the ground. She did not actually dig into the ground, but just appeared to be attacking it furiously with her front paws. Looking back, it is difficult to say now who was more stressed, at that time... me or Lucy.

At the same time I found that I was constantly asking Derek if he was alright, as he only had to twitch to get me panicking and wanting him re-admitted into hospital. The situation had been difficult enough to deal with whilst Derek Junior had been with me, but then when he returned to England, I felt on edge all the time and felt I was playing a waiting game, but waiting for what?

I did no training with the dogs, which was having a marked effect on Lucy. She was becoming more and more disobedient and was starting to disrupt the other dogs with her restless behavior indoors. I still felt that if I were to attempt any form of training, whilst feeling like I did, then I would probably do much more harm than good. All I could do was to ignore her and wait until such time as we had re-established a more orderly and settled household routine.

Things didn't settle down that quickly, and we were well into the second week of January before I felt that there was some positive progress being made. Derek could still do very little and was not allowed to drive. I also had to take over the cooking. As I have said before, since we have been together, Derek had always taken charge of all the cooking and shopping for all the various provisions we needed. It was something that he had always enjoyed doing, having been a chef when he was in the Army, in charge of the Officers Mess, which meant that he was used to arranging menus, ordering provisions and all the other things necessary for the smooth running of the mess. On the other hand, it is no secret that I have never liked cooking and freely admit that my kitchen skills are hopeless.

Thus, finding myself responsible for our meals came as a shock to my system. Since leaving the hospital, having also had the chest infection, his appetite was not particularly good and presenting him with my mixture of culinary delights did not seem to be helping matters at all.

At that time Derek was experiencing many problems, so we had to consult Dr Mike on more than one occasion for his help and assistance. He showed us both extreme patience and understanding and did so much to boost Derek's spirits with his positive outlook.

We gradually were able to return to a more settled way of life. On New Year's Day an unexpected event took place... Lucy attacked Jimmy! I was not present at the time to know what had triggered the attack. I was as surprised as Jimmy appeared to be. He did not retaliate and she did no damage. It did give me the kick start to begin training and working the dogs again. The following day I started the Heelwork to Music with Lucy, and she became very excited. She was very keen to perform all her various moves and obviously got great pleasure from doing so.

Then, another interesting thing happened a couple of days later. After our evening meal, the dogs would come and rest in the lounge. Jimmy liked to stretch out, in front of the fire. He took up his usual position and then Lucy came in, lay down beside him and rested her head on his shoulder. He lifted his head slightly to look at her, but settled again and they both then slept in that position. I never thought that I would see Lucy doing anything like that. In fact it has been the only time she has ever made contact with him in that way. It was an unexpected move, considering her behavior towards him only two days earlier.

On 17th January Lucy had her first taste of snow and was not impressed! Jimmy and Sunny loved the snow and had great fun playing, but Lucy tip toed everywhere looking very miserable.

Fortunately the snow did not last very long, as Derek's appointment in Galway had been scheduled for 25th January. He was due to see the Consultant of the Vascular Team at the University Hospital. We were both very nervous as to what the diagnosis and prognosis might be, and we were rather deflated when the day came and went, leaving us none the wiser.

It transpired that further tests were required by the Consultant, who would then make a further appointment to discuss matters in greater detail. So there was nothing more that we could do but to carry on as normal and remain optimistic.

Lucy had become calmer and I tried to encourage her to play with a ball. She was eager to run after it, but lost interest very quickly. She would not play at all if either Sunny or Jimmy were present.

We were now at the end of a year I would never forget. A time that had really brought home to me just how fragile our lives are. Oh to be as lucky as a dog, to be able to live for the moment and not dwell on the past, or worry about the future.

At the start of February I received a phone call from Suzie, that I found a little disconcerting. Apparently a young collie had been found living rough by a canal. Suzie asked me if I would have a look at him. A couple, who we got to know as Susan and Vitya, had managed, with great difficulty, to entice him into their home. They could not keep him because they were leaving the country to travel.

They brought him over to see me, but after two visits I knew that it would be impossible to rehabilitate him in the short time remaining before their departure. Over the course of the next two weeks Derek and I had many discussions about Smokey, as he had been named. We eventually decided to adopt him ourselves. Little did we realise at that time, the severity of his problems.

During the following months Smokey presented many challenges for us to overcome. So another young and extremely problematic dog joined our family.

Meanwhile Lucy continued to develop, with unexpected results. It is with great sadness that I have to say that Jimmy, who was only four years old, had to be put to sleep. Another good friend lost, but another one who left me with so many happy memories.

We are all travellers following our separate paths in life. My own journey has been enriched by the presence of the dogs that have allowed me to share their company and friendship, as we have walked side by side.

I would like to share my further experiences with you all, about our new family members and of course Lucy's progress … but that's another story.

# A Journey's End

The two of you had stood together
As soul mates always do.
Both lost and tired and trusting none
But your inner strength shone through.

Days go by; from your past you are free
Memories deep in your world of silence.
Every stranger's face that you see
Reminds you friendship just means violence.

I hoped that I might reach you,
In your lonely silent world.
Guide you and show you what to do,
Show kindness and words you'd never heard.

Slowly, quietly the trust crept in,
The calm before the storm.
Did I really think that I could begin
To change dark for a bright new dawn?

Lucy, scared of all movement and sound,
Eyes clouded with memories and pain.
I wanted to change your world around
Bring you happiness, sunshine, not rain.

Molly, you were the different one,
Older and wiser maybe?
What took place in your secret world?
That no one else could see.

The day dawned bright and clear,
A day full of promise and fun.
It should never have ended in tears,
Oh Molly what have you done?

You went on a rampage and killed,
No one would ever know why.
My heart was breaking, my eyes filled with tears
But just too numb to cry.

I thought that I had done my best,
Had left no stone unturned
But as I laid my old dog to rest,
My heavy heart returned.

The morning we said goodbye,
Your bright eyes shone like a star.
You fought so hard and you really did try
But you'd taken a step too far.

Lucy's pitiful howls haunted me that night.
Would she ever trust me again?
Could I ever make things right?
Could I ever ease her pain?

Weeks went by and then one day
She nuzzled my hand and watched  me.
This small step then opened the way,
Was she trying to make me see?

From that day forth our friendship formed,
We found the trust we'd need,
To form that very special bond
Like the planting of a seed.

It's been a rough and rocky road,
From the mountains and the night.
A journey that has taken us,
To the valley of the light.

We'll grow together you and I,
We'll trust and love and care.
At one at last, forever,
The days ahead we'll share.

*Christine Bowyer*

# Acknowledgements

Two years ago there was nothing further from my mind than writing a book and it would never have been accomplished at all, if not for the time and effort that my husband dedicated to typing out my handwritten script and his input into the presentation and constant encouragement, despite feeling unwell and in great discomfort at times. An amazing achievement on his part.

Derek would not have had the incentive or the ability to do this without the great care, patience and understanding that our own Doctor, Michael Fox, has given Derek. Without him this book would never have been written.

I thank my son Derek for staying with me and supporting me at one of the most frightening times of my life and his continued reassurance and support. Also his patience in taking Lucy's photograph for the front and back cover and his idea which led to the design.

To my daughter Suzanne, who lives abroad and has not had the opportunity to get to know Lucy, but helped me by being in constant telephone contact when her Dad was ill.

To Suzie Brown, my good friend and veterinary surgeon, who despite thinking I was nuts (her quote!), supported everything I did and was always available when I needed her help or advice. Her care of all my dogs has been exemplary. Also a big thank you for her perseverance and timing in taking the smaller photo of Lucy for the front cover.

To Darren Carr, my friend and veterinary surgeon, who took the time and patience to take the photographs of Lucy's performance at the show and the the video of our trial run. Also for his help and advice with dogs that I work with, that have physical as well as behavioural problems.

To my dear friend Sue Paling, who gave up her day to be with me when Derek had his stroke. That meant such a lot to me and I will always be grateful.

Thank you to Maureen Scanlon, who was involved in the rescue of Lucy and Molly and became a friend when the two girls first came to me and was there for me when Molly had to be put to sleep.

To Sinead O'Donohoe, my friend and veterinary nurse at the Green Veterinary Clinic, for being there on that day and working with me when problem dogs are in her care.

A very big thank you to Jennifer Quinn of Avenir Design, for designing the front cover and to both Jennifer and David for editing and presenting the book for me.

To our very dear friend Don, who sadly passed away just before the book was published. His courage was an example to everyone.

Finally, many thanks to all my friends and colleagues, too numerous to mention, for just being there.

Lightning Source UK Ltd.
Milton Keynes UK
UKOW05f1242150916

283048UK00016B/194/P